　本書は第一学習社発行の英語教科書「Vivid English Communication I」に完全準拠したワークブックです。本課は各パート見開き2ページで，教科書本文を使って「聞く」「読む」「話す(やり取り)」「話す(発表)」「書く」の4技能5領域の力を育成する問題をバランスよく用意しました。

本書の構成と利用法

【教科書本文】

● 新出単語を太字で示しました。

● 教科書に印字されていない部分(リスニングスクリプト)には網かけして示しています。

● 意味のまとまりごとにスラッシュを入れました。ここで示した意味のまとまりや，英語の強弱のリズムやイントネーションなどに注意して，本文を流暢に音読できるようにしましょう。「スピーキング・トレーナー」を使って，自分の発言を後から確認したり，発話の流暢さ(1分あたりの発話語数：words per minute)を算出することができます。発話の流暢さは70〜100wpm を目指しましょう。

📖 Reading

● 大学入学共通テストなどの形式に対応した，本文の内容理解問題です。

✏️ Vocabulary & Grammar

● 英検®や GTEC®の形式に対応した，本文中の単語，表現，文法事項についての問題です。

🎧 Listening

● 本文内容やテーマに関連した英文の聞き取り問題です。大学入学共通テストの形式に対応しています。

● ◉━○ は別売の音声 CD のトラック番号を示します。二次元コードを読み取って，音声を PC やスマートフォンなどから聞くこともできます。

💬 Interaction

● 本文内容やテーマに関連した会話などを聞いて，最後に投げかけられた質問に対して自分の考えなどを応答し，やり取りを完成させる発話問題です。

✍️💬 Production

● 本文を読んだ感想や，自分の考えや意見などを話したり書いたりして伝える問題です。

◆「知識・技能」や「思考力・判断力・表現力」を養成することを意識し，設問ごとに主に対応する観点を示しました。

◆ライティング，スピーキング問題を自分で採点できるようにしています。

　別冊『解答・解説集』の「ルーブリック評価表」(ある観点における学習の到達度を判断する基準)を用いて，自分の記述内容や発言内容を採点できます。

CONTENTS

CAN-DO List
知識・技能

Lesson 1	**#Share Your World** pp. 4-9	☐現在・過去・未来, 助動詞や, 語・連語・慣用表現について理解を深め, これらを適切に活用することができる。 ☐強弱のリズムを理解して音読することができる。
Lesson 2	**I Was Drinking Chocolate!** pp. 10-15	☐進行形, 不定詞, 動名詞や, 語・連語・慣用表現について理解を深め, これらを適切に活用することができる。 ☐強弱のリズムを理解して音読することができる。
Lesson 3	**Inspiration on the Ice** pp. 16-21	☐S + V + O (= that-節), 現在完了形, 受け身や, 語・連語・慣用表現について理解を深め, これらを適切に活用することができる。 ☐強弱のリズムを理解して音読することができる。
Lesson 4	**Esports' Time Has Arrived** pp. 22-27	☐比較 (比較級・最上級・原級), S + V + O + to-不定詞や, 語・連語・慣用表現について理解を深め, これらを適切に活用することができる。 ☐イントネーションを理解して音読することができる。
Lesson 5	**Mansai, *Kyogen* Performer** pp. 28-33	☐分詞(現在分詞・過去分詞), It is ... (for A) to ～や, 語・連語・慣用表現について理解を深め, これらを適切に活用することができる。 ☐イントネーションを理解して音読することができる。
Lesson 6	***In this Corner of the World*** pp. 34-41	☐現在完了進行形, 関係代名詞 (主格・目的格), S + V + O (=疑問詞節)や, 語・連語・慣用表現について理解を深め, これらを適切に活用することができる。 ☐イントネーションを理解して音読することができる。
Lesson 7	**Should Stores Stay Open for 24 Hours?** pp. 42-49	☐S + V + O + O (= that-節), 助動詞＋受け身, 関係代名詞 what, 過去完了形や, 語・連語・慣用表現について理解を深め, これらを適切に活用することができる。 ☐音の変化を理解して音読することができる。
Lesson 8	**Our Future with Artificial Intelligence** pp. 50-57	☐some ／ others, 分詞構文, 関係副詞 (where, when, why, how)や, 語・連語・慣用表現について理解を深め, これらを適切に活用することができる。 ☐音の変化を理解して音読することができる。
Lesson 9	**Stop Microplastic Pollution!** pp. 58-65	☐S + V + O + C (=原形不定詞・現在分詞), 条件を表す if-節, 仮定法過去や, 語・連語・慣用表現について理解を深め, これらを適切に活用することができる。 ☐シャドーイングをすることができる。
Optional Lesson	**A Retrieved Reformation** pp. 66-70	☐文構造・文法事項や, 語・連語・慣用表現について理解を深め, これらを適切に活用することができる。 ☐シャドーイングをすることができる。
Additional Lesson 1 ～ 9 pp. 71-79		☐文構造・文法事項や, 語・連語・慣用表現について理解を深め, これらを適切に活用することができる。 ☐シャドーイングをすることができる。

思考力・判断力・表現力

- [ ] 📖 SNS のメリットやデメリットについて的確に理解し，その内容を整理することができる。
- [ ] 🎧 高校生活や SNS に関する短い英文を聞いて，必要な情報を把握することができる。
- [ ] 💬 部活動や SNS について，適切に情報や考えを伝え合うことができる。
- [ ] 🗣 高校生活や SNS について，自分の考えを話して伝えることができる。
- [ ] ✍ SNS について，自分の考えを書いて伝えることができる。

- [ ] 📖 チョコレートの歴史について的確に理解し，その内容を整理することができる。
- [ ] 🎧 チョコレートに関する短い英文を聞いて，必要な情報を把握することができる。
- [ ] 💬 チョコレートについて，適切に情報や考えを伝え合うことができる。
- [ ] ✍ チョコレートについて，自分の考えを書いて伝えることができる。

- [ ] 📖 羽生結弦選手の活躍について的確に理解し，その内容を整理することができる。
- [ ] 🎧 羽生結弦選手に関する短い英文を聞いて，必要な情報を把握することができる。
- [ ] 💬 フィギュアスケートや慈善活動について，適切に情報や考えを伝え合うことができる。
- [ ] ✍ フィギュアスケートや羽生結弦選手について，自分の考えを書いて伝えることができる。

- [ ] 📖 e スポーツの特徴について的確に理解し，その内容を整理することができる。
- [ ] 🎧 e スポーツに関する短い英文を聞いて，必要な情報を把握することができる。
- [ ] 💬 e スポーツや特殊な授業や将来の夢について，適切に情報や考えを伝え合うことができる。
- [ ] 🗣 e スポーツについて，自分の考えを話して伝えることができる。
- [ ] ✍ e スポーツについて，自分の考えを書いて伝えることができる。

- [ ] 📖 野村萬斎さんの活躍について的確に理解し，その内容を整理することができる。
- [ ] 🎧 狂言に関する短い英文を聞いて，必要な情報を把握することができる。
- [ ] 💬 狂言や子どものころから続けていることや伝統文化について，適切に情報や考えを伝え合うことができる。
- [ ] 🗣 狂言について，自分の考えを話して伝えることができる。
- [ ] ✍ 狂言や伝統芸能について，自分の考えを書いて伝えることができる。

- [ ] 📖 『この世界の片隅に』の特徴について的確に理解し，その内容を整理することができる。
- [ ] 🎧 映画や戦争に関する短い英文を聞いて，必要な情報を把握することができる。
- [ ] 💬 映画や戦争について，適切に情報や考えを伝え合うことができる。
- [ ] 🗣 映画について，自分の考えを話して伝えることができる。
- [ ] ✍ 映画や日常生活や平和について，自分の考えを書いて伝えることができる。

- [ ] 📖 24時間営業店舗のメリット・デメリットや歴史について的確に理解し，その内容を整理することができる。
- [ ] 🎧 24時間営業店舗に関する短い英文を聞いて，必要な情報を把握することができる。
- [ ] 💬 24時間営業店舗や少子高齢化について，適切に情報や考えを伝え合うことができる。
- [ ] 🗣 24時間営業店舗や食品ロスについて，自分の考えを話して伝えることができる。
- [ ] ✍ 買い物について，自分の考えを書いて伝えることができる。

- [ ] 📖 AI の特徴や活用事例について的確に理解し，その内容を整理することができる。
- [ ] 🎧 AI に関する短い英文を聞いて，必要な情報を把握することができる。
- [ ] 💬 ロボットや AI について，適切に情報や考えを伝え合うことができる。
- [ ] ✍ AI について，自分の考えを書いて伝えることができる。

- [ ] 📖 海洋プラスチック汚染について的確に理解し，その内容を整理することができる。
- [ ] 🎧 プラスチックごみ問題に関する短い英文を聞いて，必要な情報を把握することができる。
- [ ] 💬 海洋汚染や環境問題について，適切に情報や考えを伝え合うことができる。
- [ ] 🗣 プラスチック問題について，自分の考えを話して伝えることができる。
- [ ] ✍ ごみ問題について，自分の考えを書いて伝えることができる。

- [ ] 📖 ストーリーの展開を的確に理解し，その内容を整理することができる。

- [ ] 📖 英文の内容を的確に理解し，整理することができる。

(POSTED by)   Manabu //

   Today was a fantastic day. // We had our entrance ceremony. // Now, / I'm a student / at Daiichi High School. // I studied very hard / and entered this school. // I'm glad / that Takashi and I / go to the same school / again. //

5 3 **Comments** //

Takashi: I'm glad, / too. // Today was a great day. // Let's have fun together! //

   Manabu@Takashi: Yeah! // I'm happy / that you are here / with me. //

Vivian: **Congratulations**! // Have an exciting school life! //

   Manabu@Vivian: Thanks! // See you. //

10 David: **Congrats**! // The cherry blossoms / in your photo / are very beautiful. //

   Manabu@David: Thank you. //

(80 words)

🔊)) 音読しよう 📖   スピーキング・トレーナー

Practice 1 スラッシュ位置で文を区切って読んでみよう ☐
Practice 2 英語の強弱のリズムに注意して読んでみよう ☐
TRY! 1分5秒以内に本文全体を音読しよう ☐

📖 **Reading** 本文の内容を読んで理解しよう【知識・技能】【思考力・判断力・表現力】   共通テスト GTEC®

Make the correct choice to complete each sentence or answer each question.   (各5点)

(1) What does "fantastic" mean in line 2? ☐
     ① cheap   ② important   ③ terrible   ④ wonderful
(2) Manabu studied hard to ☐.
     ① enter Daiichi High School
     ② have fun with Vivian and David
     ③ take an examination
     ④ take pictures of cherry blossoms
(3) Who went to the same school as Manabu? ☐
     ① David   ② David and Takashi
     ③ Takashi   ④ Vivian

🏷 Vocabulary & Grammar　重要表現や文法事項について理解しよう【知識】　英検® GTEC®

Make the correct choice to complete each sentence.　（各3点）

(1) Only a few family members attended her graduation (　　　).

① act　　　　　　② ceremony　　　　　③ festival　　　　　④ show

(2) We all were very glad (　　　) our team won the finals.

① and　　　　　　② if　　　　　　　　③ that　　　　　　④ to

(3) Since this new video game was very (　　　), I sat up late last night.

① excite　　　　　② excited　　　　　③ excites　　　　　④ exciting

(4) The children had great (　　　) at the amusement park.

① care　　　　　　② effort　　　　　　③ fun　　　　　　④ happiness

(5) She (　　　) a lot of vegetables every day.

① ate　　　　　　② eats　　　　　　③ is eating　　　　④ was eating

🎧 Listening　英文を聞いて理解しよう【知識・技能】【思考力・判断力・表現力】　共通テスト 💿2

Listen to the English and make the best choice to match the content.　（4点）

① They are going to go to different high schools.

② They went to different junior high schools.

③ They were students in the same high school.

💬 Interaction　英文を聞いて会話を続けよう【知識・技能】【思考力・判断力・表現力】　スピーキング・トレーナー 💿3

Listen to the English and respond to the last remark.　（7点）

〔メ モ 　　　　　　　　　　　　　　　　　　　　　　　　　　　　　　　　 〕

🎧 **Hints**
sports team：Basketball Team（バスケットボール部）, Track and Field Club（陸上部）, Volleyball Team（バレーボール部）
cultural club：Art Club（美術部）, Brass Band（吹奏楽部）, Calligraphy Club（書道部）, Drama Club（演劇部）

🗣 Production（Speaking）　自分の考えを話して伝えよう【思考力・判断力・表現力】　スピーキング・トレーナー

Answer the following question.　（9点）

What do you want to do in your high school life?

〔メ モ 　　　　　　　　　　　　　　　　　　　　　　　　　　　　　　　　 〕

🎧 **Hints**
I want to ～や I would like to ～で始めて，高校生活でやりたいことや成し遂げたい目標などを話しましょう。

#Share Your World

Social **media** are an important part / of our daily lives / today. // In fact, / these useful tools / make our lives very exciting. // However, / keep some rules in mind / when you use social media. //

First, / pay attention / to personal **privacy**. // Don't post **private** information / about you and your friends. // If a bad person finds the information, / you and your friends / will have some problems. //

5

Second, / don't use social media / for many hours / every day. // You will easily become a social media **addict**. // Sometimes / put down your smartphone / and look at the real world / with your own eyes. //

(95 words)

🔊 音読しよう 📖 ～～～～～～ スピーキング・トレーナー

Practice 1 スラッシュ位置で文を区切って読んでみよう ☐
Practice 2 英語の強弱のリズムに注意して読んでみよう ☐
TRY! 1分15秒以内に本文全体を音読しよう ☐

📖 **Reading** 本文の内容を読んで理解しよう【知識・技能】【思考力・判断力・表現力】 共通テスト GTEC®

Make the correct choice to complete each sentence or answer each question. (各5点)

(1) What does "personal" mean in line 4? ☐
　① complex　　　② individual　　　③ popular　　　④ various

(2) If you use social media for a lot of hours every day, you will ☐.
　① easily become an addict
　② look at the real world differently
　③ pay attention to personal data easily
　④ put down your smartphone easily

(3) Which of the following is true? ☐
　① If you use social media, you will certainly have some problems.
　② You should keep some rules in mind when you post private information.
　③ You should post personal information about either you or your friends.
　④ You shouldn't post personal information about you and your friends.

🔊 英語の強弱のリズムを理解して音読することができる。　📖 SNS に関する英文を読んで概要や要点をとらえることができる。
📝 文脈を理解して適切な語句を用いて英文を完成することができる。　🎧 平易な英語で話される短い英文を聞いて必要な情報を聞き取ることができる。
💬 SNS について簡単な語句を用いて情報や考えを伝えることができる。　💬 スマートフォンについて簡単な語句を用いて考えを表現することができる。

🏷 Vocabulary & Grammar　重要表現や文法事項について理解しよう【知識】　英検® GTEC®

Make the correct choice to complete each sentence. （各3点）

(1) It was cold last night. (　　　　), there was a frost.
　① At first　　　　② At last　　　　③ In conclusion　　　　④ In fact

(2) As Jack is always poker-faced, I don't know what he has in (　　　　).
　① brain　　　　② head　　　　③ heart　　　　④ mind

(3) This is my first trip to Japan. Please give me (　　　　) about Kyoto.
　① any informations　② informations　③ some information　④ some informations

(4) I put my bag (　　　　) on the floor to answer my phone.
　① down　　　　② into　　　　③ out　　　　④ up

(5) Look! The sky is getting dark. I think it (　　　　).
　① is going to rain　② is raining　③ rained　④ rains

🎧 Listening　英文を聞いて理解しよう【知識・技能】【思考力・判断力・表現力】　共通テスト 💿4

Listen to the English and make the best choice to match the content. （4点）

① The speaker warns that we should be careful about our remarks on social media.
② When using social media, we don't have to be careful about our remarks because we can completely delete them later.
③ When using social media, we must remember that we can easily delete our remarks.

💬 Interaction　英文を聞いて会話を続けよう【知識・技能】【思考力・判断力・表現力】　スピーキング・トレーナー 💿5

Listen to the English and respond to the last remark. （7点）

〔メ モ　　　　　　　　　　　　　　　　　　　　　　　　　　　　　　　　　〕

🎧 **Hints**
　1日に SNS に費やす時間を考えて話しましょう。

💬 Production (Speaking)　自分の考えを話して伝えよう【思考力・判断力・表現力】　スピーキング・トレーナー

Answer the following question. （9点）

Do you think that smartphones will cause some bad effects on our daily lives? Why?

〔メ モ　　　　　　　　　　　　　　　　　　　　　　　　　　　　　　　　　〕

🎧 **Hints**
　Yes の場合は悪影響の理由を，No の場合はスマートフォンの利点を答えましょう。

How do you use social media? // You can share **recent** events / in your everyday life / with your friends. // You can also introduce your favorite shops / and interesting Internet news. //

On social media, / you can talk / about some social problems, / too. // 5 Sometimes / you may have an exciting **discussion** / about such problems / with your friends. //

If you use social media carefully, / they can be a wonderful tool. // You can communicate / with people / all over the world. // Now, / why don't you open up a huge new world / in the **palm** / of your hand? //

(90 words)

🔊)) **音読しよう** スピーキング・トレーナー

Practice 1 スラッシュ位置で文を区切って読んでみよう ☐
Practice 2 英語の強弱のリズムに注意して読んでみよう ☐
TRY! 1分15秒以内に本文全体を音読しよう ☐

📖 Reading 本文の内容を読んで理解しよう【知識・技能】【思考力・判断力・表現力】 （共通テスト）

Make the correct choice to complete each sentence or answer each question. （各5点）

(1) Social media can be a fantastic tool ☐ .
 ① if you don't use them carefully
 ② if you use them every day
 ③ unless you use them carefully
 ④ unless you use them carelessly

(2) On social media, ☐ .
 ① you can introduce some of your favorite shops and interesting Internet news
 ② you cannot have communication with people around the world
 ③ you must argue with your friends about social issues in the world
 ④ you must exchange recent events in your everyday life with your friends

(3) Which is the best title for the article? ☐
 ① How to Share Recent Events on Social Media
 ② How to Solve Social Problems
 ③ The Way You Make Friends on Social Media
 ④ What Can You Do on Social Media?

🔊 Vocabulary & Grammar　重要表現や文法事項について理解しよう【知識】　英検® GTEC®

Make the correct choice to complete each sentence.　（各3点）

(1) Thank you very much for sharing this important information (　　　) me.

　① across　　　　　② at　　　　　　　③ to　　　　　　　④ with

(2) I would like to introduce (　　　) Mr. Jones, an assistant language teacher.

　① for you　　　　② to you　　　　　③ you for　　　　④ you to

(3) The (　　　) about the environmental problem is still going on.

　① attention　　　② communication　③ discussion　　　④ expression

(4) Alex, you look tired. (　　　) don't you go to bed?

　① How　　　　　② When　　　　　③ Where　　　　④ Why

(5) Must I get up at six tomorrow morning? —— No, you (　　　).

　① don't　　　　② don't have to　　③ must　　　　④ must not

🎧 Listening　英文を聞いて理解しよう【知識・技能】【思考力・判断力・表現力】　共通テスト　◎ 6

Listen to the English and make the best choice to match the content.　（4点）

　① The speaker can die if she doesn't use social media.

　② The speaker can't imagine her life without social media.

　③ The speaker can't picture her life if she uses social media.

💬 Interaction　英文を聞いて会話を続けよう【知識・技能】【思考力・判断力・表現力】　スピーキング・トレーナー　◎ 7

Listen to the English and respond to the remarks.　（7点）

〔メモ 　　　　　　　　　　　　　　　　　　　　　　　　　　　　　　　〕

🔊 **Hints**
それぞれの SNS の特徴を踏まえた上で，自分の好みとその理由も含めて話しましょう。

✍ Production（Writing）　自分の考えを書いて伝えよう【思考力・判断力・表現力】

Write your answer to the following question.　（9点）

What do you think about the advantages of social media as a communication tool?

🔊 **Hints**
コミュニケーションを図る際に SNS を使えばどんなことができるか考えましょう。

I Was Drinking Chocolate!

Vivian: Hello, / Kumi! //

Kumi: Hi, / Vivian! // Welcome / to my house. // Come in! //

Vivian: Thank you. // What were you doing, / Kumi? //

Kumi: I was drinking chocolate. //

5 *Vivian:* Oh, / I like hot chocolate! // It really tastes good! //

Kumi: Um ... / do you know / about the long history / of chocolate? //

Vivian: I don't know much / about it. // Please tell me. //

Kumi: Actually, / people drank chocolate / from very ancient times. // People first ate chocolate bars / around 1850. //

10 *Vivian:* Is that right? //

Kumi: Yeah. // Manabu and I / are working / on a project / about the history / of chocolate / for an English class. //

Vivian: Are you going to give a **presentation** / in class? //

Kumi: Yes. // So / we have to make some good **slides**. //

(103 words)

音読しよう

スピーキング・トレーナー

Practice 1 スラッシュ位置で文を区切って読んでみよう ☐

Practice 2 英語の強弱のリズムに注意して読んでみよう ☐

TRY! 1分20秒以内に本文全体を音読しよう ☐

Reading 本文の内容を読んで理解しよう【知識・技能】【思考力・判断力・表現力】

共通テスト GTEC®

Make the correct choice to complete each sentence or answer each question. （各5点[(3)は完答]）

(1) What does "ancient" mean in line 8? ☐

① current　　② modern　　③ normal　　④ old

(2) Kumi told Vivian that ☐.

① people ate chocolate bars for the first time around 1850

② people ate chocolate bars from very ancient times

③ people drank chocolate for the first time around 1850

④ she was eating chocolate bars for the first time

(3) According to the dialogue you read, which of the following are true? (Choose two options. The order does not matter.) ☐ · ☐

① Kumi and Manabu are going to give a presentation about the history of chocolate.

② Kumi and Vivian are working on a project about the history of chocolate.

③ Kumi is working on a project about the history of chocolate.

④ Manabu and Vivian are working on a project about the history of chocolate.

🏷 Vocabulary & Grammar 重要表現や文法事項について理解しよう【知識】 英検® GTEC®

Make the correct choice to complete each sentence. （各3点）

(1) Tourists are (　　　) by our staff members at the gate and shown where to go.
　① meeting　　　　② met　　　　　　③ welcomed　　　　④ welcoming

(2) Generally, Americans regard slurping as very rude when they (　　　) soup in a restaurant.
　① bring　　　　　② eat　　　　　　③ get　　　　　　　④ take

(3) She is working (　　　) a crossword puzzle.
　① for　　　　　　② in　　　　　　　③ on　　　　　　　④ with

(4) I'm going to ask each of you to (　　　) a short presentation.
　① get　　　　　　② give　　　　　　③ open　　　　　　④ take

(5) Kumi fell and broke her leg while she (　　　).
　① is skating　　　② skated　　　　③ skates　　　　　④ was skating

🎧 Listening 英文を聞いて理解しよう【知識・技能】【思考力・判断力・表現力】 共通テスト ● 8

Listen to the English and make the best choice to match the content. （4点）
　① The speaker doesn't like eating chocolate bars.
　② The speaker likes cacao beans.
　③ The speaker now knows that chocolate is made from cacao beans.

💬 Interaction 英文を聞いて会話を続けよう【知識・技能】【思考力・判断力・表現力】 スピーキング・トレーナー ● 9

Listen to the English and respond to the last remark. （7点）
　〔メ モ　　　　　　　　　　　　　　　　　　　　　　　　　　　　　　　　　　　　　〕

🎧 **Hints**
　Why don't you ～? という提案に対して自分の考えを伝えましょう。

✍ Production (Writing) 自分の考えを書いて伝えよう【思考力・判断力・表現力】

Write your answer to the following question. （9点）
Have you ever drunk chocolate?

🎧 **Hints**
　チョコレートを飲んだことがある人は，その経験について書きましょう。そうでない人は，その理由などについて書きましょう。

I Was Drinking Chocolate!

Kumi: Today, / we want / to talk / about the history / of chocolate. // Over 3,000 years ago, / people / in Central America / first had wild **cacao** beans. // People there / started / to grow cacao trees. //

Manabu: From about 250 / to 900 AD, / the Maya used wild cacao beans / as
5　　money. // They used them / in events / for the gods, / too. // Cacao beans were very **precious**. //

Kumi: From about 1200 / to 1500, / the Aztecs used cacao beans / to pay **taxes**. // In the 16th century, / people / in Spain / found this: / Chocolate is good / for people's health. //

10 *Manabu:* They put sugar / and milk / into the chocolate drink. // It tasted good. // Then, / an Englishman made the first **solid** chocolate / around 1850. //

(108 words)

🔊 **音読しよう** 📖 ～～～～～ スピーキング・トレーナー

Practice 1 スラッシュ位置で文を区切って読んでみよう ☐
Practice 2 英語の強弱のリズムに注意して読んでみよう ☐
TRY! 1分25秒以内に本文全体を音読しよう ☐

📖 **Reading** 本文の内容を読んで理解しよう【知識・技能】【思考力・判断力・表現力】　　共通テスト GTEC®

Make the correct choice to complete each sentence or answer each question. （各5点[(3)は完答]）

(1) What does "precious" mean in line 6? ☐
　① cheap　　　　　② useless　　　　　③ valuable　　　　　④ wide

(2) ☐, the Spanish found that chocolate was good for people's health.
　① Around 1850　　　　　　　　　② From about 1200 to 1500
　③ From about 250 to 900 AD　　　④ In the 16th century

(3) Put the following events (①～④) into the order in which they happened.
　☐→☐→☐→☐
　① People in Central America started to grow cacao trees.
　② People in Spain put sugar and milk into the chocolate drink.
　③ The Aztecs used cacao beans to pay taxes.
　④ The Maya used wild cacao beans in events for the gods.

Goals

🔊 英語の強弱のリズムを理解して音読することができる。 📖 チョコレートの歴史に関するプレゼンテーションを読んで概要や要点をとらえることができる。
📝 文脈を理解して適切な語句を用いて英文を完成することができる。 🎧 平易な英語で話される短い英文を聞いて必要な情報を聞き取ることができる。
💬 チョコレートについて簡単な語句を用いて情報や考えを伝えることができる。 ✍ チョコレートについて簡単な語句を用いて考えを表現することができる。

Vocabulary & Grammar 　重要表現や文法事項について理解しよう【知識】　　（英検®）（GTEC®）

Make the correct choice to complete each sentence. （各3点）

(1) A good medicine (　　　) bitter.

① feels　　　　　② looks　　　　　③ sounds　　　　　④ tastes

(2) Does the price include (　　　) and service charges?

① bill　　　　　② change　　　　　③ money　　　　　④ tax

(3) I think of Taro (　　　) a good friend.

① about　　　　　② as　　　　　③ on　　　　　④ to

(4) Water that has frozen into a (　　　) state is called "ice."

① cold　　　　　② gas　　　　　③ liquid　　　　　④ solid

(5) Bob came to New York in order (　　　) for a job.

① look　　　　　② looking　　　　　③ to look　　　　　④ to looking

 ## Listening 　英文を聞いて理解しよう【知識・技能】【思考力・判断力・表現力】　　（共通テスト） 10

Listen to the English and make the best choice to match the content. （4点）

① Chocolate is known as a health food.

② Chocolate is regarded only as a snack.

③ The speaker doesn't know that chocolate contains vitamins.

 ## Interaction 　英文を聞いて会話を続けよう【知識・技能】【思考力・判断力・表現力】　（スピーキング・トレーナー） 11

Listen to the English and respond to the last remark. （7点）

〔メモ 　　〕

🎤 **Hints**
Yes か No だけではなく，理由なども含めて話しましょう。

 ## Production（Writing） 　自分の考えを書いて伝えよう【思考力・判断力・表現力】

Write your answer to the following question. （9点）

Write about some benefits of eating chocolate for our health.

🎤 **Hints**
チョコレートを食べることによる健康上の利点について具体的に説明しましょう。

Kumi: Now, / we want / to hear your questions / about our presentation. //

Takashi: What events / did the Maya use cacao beans / for? //

Manabu: For their birth, / **marriage** / and death ceremonies. // People **offered** cacao beans / to the gods. //

5 *Taro:* Is chocolate really good / for our health? // Can you tell us more / about this? //

Kumi: People / in Spain / drank chocolate / as a health food. // Sick people took it / as medicine. // Um ... / any other questions? //

Vivian: I want / to buy some nice chocolate / for my host mother. // What do

10 you **recommend**? //

Kumi: How about getting 100% cacao chocolate? // It's not so sweet, / but it's very healthy! //

(95 words)

音読しよう　　　　　　　　　　　　　　スピーキング・トレーナー

Practice 1 スラッシュ位置で文を区切って読んでみよう ☐
Practice 2 英語の強弱のリズムに注意して読んでみよう ☐
TRY! 1分15秒以内に本文全体を音読しよう ☐

Reading 本文の内容を読んで理解しよう【知識・技能】【思考力・判断力・表現力】　共通テスト GTEC®

Make the correct choice to complete each sentence or answer each question. （各5点）

(1) What does "offer" mean in line 3? ☐
　① bring　　　② get　　　③ give　　　④ take

(2) Manabu told Takashi that ☐.
　① chocolate was really good for our health
　② 100% cacao chocolate was not so sweet
　③ the Maya used cacao beans as medicine
　④ the Maya used cacao beans for their ceremonies

(3) People in Spain ☐.
　① didn't drink chocolate as a health food
　② didn't use chocolate as medicine
　③ drank chocolate as a health food
　④ loved 100% cacao chocolate

Goals

🔊 英語の強弱のリズムを理解して音読することができる。　📖 チョコレートに関する質疑応答を読んで概要や要点をとらえることができる。
📝 文脈を理解して適切な語句を用いて英文を完成することができる。　🎧 平易な英語で話される短い英文を聞いて必要な情報を聞き取ることができる。
💬 チョコレートについて簡単な語句を用いて情報や考えを伝えることができる。　✍ チョコレートについて簡単な語句を用いて考えを表現することができる。

Vocabulary & Grammar　重要表現や文法事項について理解しよう【知識】　英検® GTEC®

Make the correct choice to complete each sentence.　(各3点)

(1) I (　　　) to give them a ride home in my car.
　① advised　　　② offered　　　③ suggested　　　④ told

(2) A police officer (　　　) me to go with him to the police station.
　① said　　　② spoke　　　③ talked　　　④ told

(3) The sales staff (　　　) buying a new car, but my wife said we could not afford it.
　① claimed　　　② decided　　　③ recommended　　　④ showed

(4) This cake is too (　　　) for me.
　① cute　　　② strict　　　③ strong　　　④ sweet

(5) I'm afraid of (　　　) mistakes when I speak English.
　① having made　　　② made　　　③ make　　　④ making

🎧 Listening　英文を聞いて理解しよう【知識・技能】【思考力・判断力・表現力】　共通テスト 🔘12

Listen to the English and make the best choice to match the content.　(4点)
　① The speaker has finished making chocolates for Valentine's Day.
　② The speaker is going to make chocolates for Valentine's Day.
　③ The speaker is now busy making chocolates for Valentine's Day.

💬 Interaction　英文を聞いて会話を続けよう【知識・技能】【思考力・判断力・表現力】　スピーキング・トレーナー 🔘13

Listen to the English and respond to the last remark.　(7点)
　〔メモ　　　　　　　　　　　　　　　　　　　　　　　　　　　　　　　　　　　〕

Hints
once a week (週1回)，rarely (めったに…ない)，never (けっして…ない)などの表現を使って頻度を表すことができます。

✍ Production (Writing)　自分の考えを書いて伝えよう【思考力・判断力・表現力】

Write your answer to the following question.　(9点)
Which would you like better, bitter chocolate or milk chocolate? Why?

_____

Hints
チョコレートの味については，bitter (苦い)，sweet (甘い)などと表すことができます。

Inspiration on the Ice

Yuzuru Hanyu started skating / in Sendai / when he was four. // At first, / he didn't like practicing, / but he loved showing people / his figure skating skills. // He **developed** his skills / and won international junior **competitions** / in 2009. //

After that, / Yuzuru won **memorable medals** and **awards**. // His second
5 Olympic gold / was the 1,000th gold / in the Winter Olympics. // He was given the People's **Honor** Award / in 2018. //

Yuzuru faced many **hardships** / as well. // After the 2014 Olympics, / he **suffered** several **injuries**. // He even injured his **ankle** / shortly before the 2018 Olympics. // However, / he **trusted** himself / and always thought / about skating. //
10 Yuzuru thought / that those hardships / gave him the power / to win. //

(109 words)

音読しよう

スピーキング・トレーナー

Practice 1 スラッシュ位置で文を区切って読んでみよう ☐
Practice 2 英語の強弱のリズムに注意して読んでみよう ☐
TRY! 1分25秒以内に本文全体を音読しよう ☐

Reading 本文の内容を読んで理解しよう【知識・技能】【思考力・判断力・表現力】

共通テスト GTEC®

Make the correct choice to complete each sentence or answer each question. (各5点[(3)は完答])

(1) Shortly after Yuzuru started skating, he liked ☐.
　① developing his figure skating skills
　② performing in front of people
　③ practicing skating
　④ taking part in competitions

(2) What does "face" mean in line 7? ☐
　① avoid　　　　② cause　　　　③ encounter　　　　④ see

(3) According to the article you read, which of the following are true? (Choose two options. The order does not matter.) ☐ · ☐
　① Yuzuru got the People's Honor Award in 2009.
　② Yuzuru got the power to win through several hardships.
　③ Yuzuru got two gold medals in the Winter Olympics.
　④ Yuzuru stopped thinking about skating when he got injured.
　⑤ Yuzuru suffered injuries just after the 2018 Olympics.

🏷 Vocabulary & Grammar　重要表現や文法事項について理解しよう【知識】　(英検®) (GTEC®)

Make the correct choice to complete each sentence.　(各3点)

(1) I didn't recognize him (　　　　), but I remembered him as soon as I heard his name.

　① at first　　　　② first of all　　　　③ firstly　　　　④ for the first time

(2) Bob went to Germany and (　　　　) his skills as a doctor there.

　① developed　　　② grew　　　　③ made　　　　④ reached

(3) Our team worked hard to win the national (　　　　).

　① competition　　② conference　　③ hardship　　④ skill

(4) Lisa is a good pianist and a good singer (　　　　) well.

　① as　　　　　② even　　　　③ so　　　　④ such

(5) Some people think (　　　　) music is good for plants.

　① about　　　　② by　　　　③ of　　　　④ that

🎧 Listening　英文を聞いて理解しよう【知識・技能】【思考力・判断力・表現力】　(共通テスト) ⊙ 14

Listen to the English and make the best choice to match the content.　(4点)

　① The speaker lived in Sendai.

　② The speaker moved to Sendai in 1994.

　③ The speaker was born in Ishinomaki.

💬 Interaction　英文を聞いて会話を続けよう【知識・技能】【思考力・判断力・表現力】　スピーキング・トレーナー ⊙ 15

Listen to the English and respond to the last remark.　(7点)

〔メモ　　　　　　　　　　　　　　　　　　　　　　　　　　　　　　　　　　　〕

🎧 Hints
I like [love] ... のように文の形ではなく，好きな競技種目名だけを答えても構いません。

✍ Production (Writing)　自分の考えを書いて伝えよう【思考力・判断力・表現力】

Write your answer to the following question.　(9点)

Do you want to watch figure skating at an arena?　Why?

_____

_____

🎧 Hints
フィギュアスケートの演技については，elegant (優雅な)，powerful (力強い)などと表すことができます。

The Great East Japan Earthquake / in 2011 / was another hardship / for Yuzuru. // He was training / at his home **rink** / at the time. // Yuzuru **escaped** / from the **arena**. // Ten days later, / he started skating again / with the help of people / around him. //

5 Since then, / Yuzuru has thought about people / in **disaster** areas. // He has skated / in a lot of charity ice shows. // When he won his first Olympic gold, / he said, / "I'm here / because many people / around the world / have supported me." //

After the 2018 Olympics, / Yuzuru **paraded** / through the streets of Sendai. // 10 About 100,000 people / welcomed him. // "I'm happy / to come back here / with this gold medal," / Yuzuru said / during the ceremony. //

(112 words)

音読しよう

スピーキング・トレーナー

Practice 1 スラッシュ位置で文を区切って読んでみよう ☐
Practice 2 英語の強弱のリズムに注意して読んでみよう ☐
TRY! 1分30秒以内に本文全体を音読しよう ☐

Reading 本文の内容を読んで理解しよう【知識・技能】【思考力・判断力・表現力】 共通テスト GTEC®

Make the correct choice to complete each sentence or answer each question. （各5点）

(1) Since 2011, Yuzuru ☐.

① has never thought about people in disaster areas, but he has done many charity ice shows

② has thought about people in disaster areas, and he has done many charity ice shows

③ has thought about people in disaster areas, but he hasn't done any charity ice shows

④ hasn't thought about people in disaster areas, so he has never done any charity ice shows

(2) What does "come back" mean in line 10? ☐
① realize　　　② rely　　　③ respond　　　④ return

(3) You have learned that Yuzuru ☐.

① was happy to come back to Ishinomaki with his gold medal

② was performing in a charity ice show when the Great East Japan Earthquake happened

③ was training at his home rink when the Great East Japan Earthquake happened

④ won his first Olympic gold after he paraded through the streets of Sendai

✏ Vocabulary & Grammar　重要表現や文法事項について理解しよう【知識】　英検® GTEC®

Make the correct choice to complete each sentence.　（各3点）

(1)　We have (　　　) to walk before sunset.
　　① another miles ten　② another ten miles　③ ten another miles　④ ten miles another

(2)　You're just trying to (　　　) from reality.
　　① avoid　　　　　② escape　　　　　③ prevent　　　　　④ stay

(3)　Donations are needed months or even years after a (　　　) strikes.
　　① disaster　　　　② hardship　　　　③ problem　　　　④ victim

(4)　He had a great deal of evidence to (　　　) his story.
　　① discourage　　　② raise　　　　　③ stop　　　　　　④ support

(5)　Are Jack and Betty still living in Los Angeles? —— No, they (　　　) to New York.
　　① had just moved　② have just moved　③ just move　　　④ will have just moved

🎧 Listening　英文を聞いて理解しよう【知識・技能】【思考力・判断力・表現力】　共通テスト　🔘16

Listen to the English and make the best choice to match the content.　（4点）
　　① The speaker did some charity activities.
　　② The speaker has never taken part in charity activities.
　　③ The speaker suffered from the earthquake.

💬 Interaction　英文を聞いて会話を続けよう【知識・技能】【思考力・判断力・表現力】　スピーキング・トレーナー　🔘17

Listen to the English and respond to the last remark.　（7点）
　〔メ モ　　　　　　　　　　　　　　　　　　　　　　　　　　　　　　　　　　　　　　〕

🔑 **Hints**
　Yes の場合は自分自身の経験について，No の場合は興味のあるボランティア活動や慈善活動について話しましょう。

🖊 Production（Writing）　自分の考えを書いて伝えよう【思考力・判断力・表現力】

Write your answer to the following question.　（9点）
Why do you think Yuzuru Hanyu is loved by so many people?

🔑 **Hints**
　羽生選手のスケート演技や人柄などの観点から考えましょう。

Reporter: I'd like to ask you / about your friendship / with Javier Fernandez. //

Yuzuru: Thank you. // I'm glad / to talk about Javier / because I know / he is often asked / about me / by Japanese reporters. //

Reporter: What's he like? //

5 *Yuzuru:* He's very kind. // Too kind / to **compete**, / I think. // I won the gold medal / at the Olympics, / and he took third place. // I **wept**. // We trained together, / and I knew / he worked hard / to get a medal. // I was **proud** / of him. //

Reporter: What does he mean / to you? //

10 *Yuzuru:* He means a lot / to me. // We've always **inspired** / each other. // I got the gold / because he's been / with me. //

(102 words)

音読しよう

スピーキング・トレーナー

Practice 1 スラッシュ位置で文を区切って読んでみよう ☐
Practice 2 英語の強弱のリズムに注意して読んでみよう ☐
TRY! 1分20秒以内に本文全体を音読しよう ☐

Reading 本文の内容を読んで理解しよう【知識・技能】【思考力・判断力・表現力】

共通テスト

Make the correct choice to complete each sentence or answer each question. (各5点)

(1) What did the reporter ask Yuzuru about in the interview? ☐

① Figure skating skills.

② Friendship between Yuzuru and Javier Fernandez.

③ His performance at the Olympics.

④ The gold medal at the Olympics.

(2) One **opinion** from Yuzuru's remarks in his interview is that ☐.

① Japanese reporters often ask Javier about Yuzuru

② Javier trained hard to get a medal

③ Javier is too kind to compete

④ Yuzuru got the gold medal at the Olympics

(3) Yuzuru thinks that he got the gold medal because ☐.

① he did his best performance

② his family supported him

③ Javier has always inspired him

④ Javier was proud of Yuzuru

🏷 Vocabulary & Grammar　重要表現や文法事項について理解しよう【知識】　英検Ⓡ GTECⓇ

Make the correct choice to complete each sentence.　（各3点）

(1) Getting good grades (　　　) a lot to him.
　① avoids　　　　　② decides　　　　　③ means　　　　　④ supposes

(2) Our team has lost ten straight games.　We need a new manager who (　　　) us.
　① expresses　　　② inspires　　　　③ introduces　　　④ trusts

(3) ABC company has (　　　) with XYZ company for customers for several years.
　① competed　　　② continued　　　③ destroyed　　　④ inspired

(4) Bob is proud (　　　) the fact that his sister won first prize at the contest.
　① at　　　　　　② in　　　　　　　③ of　　　　　　　④ with

(5) Where were these pictures (　　　)?　In Hokkaido?
　① take　　　　　② taken　　　　　③ taking　　　　　④ took

🎧 Listening　英文を聞いて理解しよう【知識・技能】【思考力・判断力・表現力】　共通テスト　🔘18

Listen to the English and make the best choice to match the content.　（4点）
　① The speaker can perform all kinds of jumps in figure skating.
　② The speaker wants to perform like Yuzuru Hanyu.
　③ Yuzuru Hanyu is practicing all kinds of jumps in figure skating.

💬 Interaction　英文を聞いて会話を続けよう【知識・技能】【思考力・判断力・表現力】　スピーキング・トレーナー　🔘19

Listen to the English and respond to the remark.　（7点）
〔メ モ　　　　　　　　　　　　　　　　　　　　　　　　　　　　　　　　　　　〕

👆 **Hints**
　My favorite professional figure skater is ... や I like ... などの表現を使って話しましょう。

✍ Production（Writing）　自分の考えを書いて伝えよう【思考力・判断力・表現力】

Write your answer to the following question.　（9点）
Write about a story of your friendship between you and your friends, like the one between Yuzuru and Javier.

🎵 **Hints**
　友達との友情を感じた出来事について具体的に説明しましょう。

Esports' Time Has Arrived

There is a popular, new sport / today: / **esports**. // Esports is the short name / for "**electronic** sports." // Esports players play video games / in **individual** / or team competitions. //

In the late 20th century, / people started playing video games / for fun. // 5 Today, / many people enjoy them / in a different way. // Computers and other machines today / are smarter and cheaper / than those of the 20th century. // Also, / Internet technology has **advanced**, / so people can now compete online / with **gamers** / around the world. // They often use their own powerful machines. //

10 Many players have become very **skilled**, / and even professional players / have appeared. // Many **organizations** have started tournaments. // As a result, / such video **gaming** has gotten the name / "esports." //

(113 words)

音読しよう　　　　　　　　　　　　　　　　　スピーキング・トレーナー

Practice 1 スラッシュ位置で文を区切って読んでみよう ☐
Practice 2 イントネーションに注意して読んでみよう ☐
TRY! 1分20秒以内に本文全体を音読しよう ☐

Reading 本文の内容を読んで理解しよう【知識・技能】【思考力・判断力・表現力】　共通テスト GTEC®

Make the correct choice to complete each sentence or answer each question. （各5点）

(1) Esports players play video games ☐.
　① either in individual or team competitions
　② in individual competitions only
　③ in team competitions only
　④ neither in individual nor team competitions

(2) You have learned that ☐ in the 20th century.
　① many organizations started esports tournaments
　② people enjoyed playing video games
　③ people started video games to take part in the esports tournaments
　④ professional esports players appeared

(3) What does "organization" mean in line 11? ☐
　① action　　　　　② cell　　　　　③ institution　　　　　④ member

🏷 Vocabulary & Grammar　重要表現や文法事項について理解しよう【知識】　英検® GTEC®

Make the correct choice to complete each sentence.　（各3点）

(1) Most churches were built with donations from (　　　).

　① individual　　② individuals　　③ many individual　　④ much individuals

(2) Medical science (　　　) a great deal in the 20th century.

　① advanced　　② arrived　　③ encouraged　　④ reached

(3) She finally (　　　) when the meeting was almost over.

　① appeared　　② saw　　③ seemed　　④ showed

(4) The traffic was very heavy and (　　　) I arrived late.

　① as a result　　② as for　　③ as to　　④ as well

(5) That super car is (　　　) in the world.

　① expensive more　　② expensive the most　　③ more expensive　　④ the most expensive

🎧 Listening　英文を聞いて理解しよう【知識・技能】【思考力・判断力・表現力】　共通テスト　💿20

Listen to the English and make the best choice to match the content.　（4点）

　① High school students took part in the competition.

　② More than 1,500 teams participated in the competition.

　③ The speaker took part in the competition.

💬 Interaction　英文を聞いて会話を続けよう【知識・技能】【思考力・判断力・表現力】　スピーキング・トレーナー　💿21

Listen to the English and respond to the last remark.　（7点）

〔メ モ　　　　　　　　　　　　　　　　　　　　　　　　　　　　　　　　　　〕

🔔 Hints

I like to play [watch] ... の表現を使って好きな e スポーツゲームを答えましょう。

✍ Production（Writing）　自分の考えを書いて伝えよう【思考力・判断力・表現力】

Write your answer to the following question.　（9点）

Do you think that playing online sports games is superior to playing sports in the real world? Why?

🔔 Hints

eスポーツが通常のスポーツよりも優れている点があるか考えてみましょう。

Esports' Time Has Arrived

Esports tournaments now take place / online / or in big arenas / all over the world. // Players compete / against each other / in various games, / such as **battle** games, / card games / and sports games. //

Becoming a great esports player / is often as difficult / as becoming a
5 great player / of any other kind of sport. // For example, / players need / to **respond** quickly / and think hard / about **strategies**. // They also need good communication skills / because they often work / as a team. //

Today / in Japan, / more and more people believe / that esports will change **society**. // Some high schools have special programs / for esports. // The
10 students there / learn the **basics** / of IT / and practice / how to win games. //

(111 words)

 音読しよう

Practice 1 スラッシュ位置で文を区切って読んでみよう ☐
Practice 2 イントネーションに注意して読んでみよう ☐
TRY! 1分20秒以内に本文全体を音読しよう ☐

スピーキング・トレーナー

Reading 本文の内容を読んで理解しよう【知識・技能】【思考力・判断力・表現力】 （共通テスト）

Make the correct choice to complete each sentence or answer each question. （各5点［(3)は完答]）

(1) What is necessary for you to become a great esports player? ☐
　① To have good communication skills to change society.
　② To think hard about strategies and have good communication skills.
　③ To think hard about strategies to communicate with your enemies.
　④ To respond quickly to change society.

(2) One **opinion** from the article is that ☐.
　① esports players often work as a team
　② esports tournaments take place online or in big arenas
　③ esports will change society
　④ some high school students learn the basics of IT

(3) According to the article you read, which of the following are true? (Choose two options. The order does not matter.) ☐ · ☐
　① Becoming a great esports player is more difficult than becoming a great player of any other sport.
　② Becoming a great esports player isn't easy.
　③ Esports tournaments take place all over the world.
　④ Most high schools in Japan teach students the basics of IT and how to win esports games.
　⑤ Only professional players can take part in esports tournaments.

🏷 Vocabulary & Grammar 重要表現や文法事項について理解しよう【知識】 英検® GTEC®

Make the correct choice to complete each sentence. （各3点）

(1) Many students didn't know that the Civil War (　　　) between 1861 and 1865.
① has taken place　② takes place　③ took place　④ was taken place

(2) Tom and Mary met (　　　) for the first time while jogging in Central Park.
① each other　② for each other　③ in each other　④ with each other

(3) The baby (　　　) by smiling.
① reached　② realized　③ reduced　④ responded

(4) The (　　　) of surfing are easy to learn.
① advantages　② basics　③ competitions　④ tasks

(5) My sister has (　　　) I have.
① as books many as　② as many as books　③ as many books as　④ books as many as

🎧 Listening 英文を聞いて理解しよう【知識・技能】【思考力・判断力・表現力】 共通テスト 💿22

Listen to the English and make the best choice to match the content. （4点）
① The speaker belongs to the esports club.
② The speaker doesn't like esports.
③ The speaker wants to be a member of the esports club.

💬 Interaction 英文を聞いて会話を続けよう【知識・技能】【思考力・判断力・表現力】 スピーキング・トレーナー 💿23

Listen to the English and respond to the last remark. （7点）
〔メモ　　　　　　　　　　　　　　　　　　　　　　　　　　　　　　　　　　　〕

🔑**Hints**
主要教科以外にどのような特殊な授業があるか(No の場合は，どのような特殊な授業を学びたいか)を話しましょう。

✍ Production（Writing） 自分の考えを書いて伝えよう【思考力・判断力・表現力】

Write your answer to the following question. （9点）
What do you think are positive effects for children from playing esports?

🔑**Hints**
本文第2段落の内容も参考にして書きましょう。

I'm 15. // I love esports. // I hope / to become a good esports player. // It's my future dream. // But my parents don't want me / to become an esports player. // They say / playing computer games / is only a waste / of time. // Am I wrong? //

Answer //

5 I live / in South Korea. // I'm working hard / to become a professional esports player. // You have the same dream, / too, / right? // Then, / learn the following things. //

    1. Be strong and healthy / — **physically** and **mentally.** //

    2. Improve your language skills / — especially English skills. //

10   3. **Cultivate** your spirit / of fair play. //

I know / these are not easy. // But / if you work hard, / your parents will understand you. //

(107 words)

音読しよう

スピーキング・トレーナー

Practice 1 スラッシュ位置で文を区切って読んでみよう ☐
Practice 2 イントネーションに注意して読んでみよう ☐
TRY! 1分15秒以内に本文全体を音読しよう ☐

Reading 本文の内容を読んで理解しよう【知識・技能】【思考力・判断力・表現力】 共通テスト

Make the correct choice to complete each sentence or answer each question. （各5点）

(1) The Japanese boy wants to become an esports player, ☐.
  ① and his parents also want to   ② and his parents are for it
  ③ but his parents are against it   ④ but his parents don't want to

(2) From the Internet site, you have learned that the Japanese boy ☐.
  ① gets some advice to become a good esports player
  ② gives some advice to his parents
  ③ has a friend who is a professional esports player
  ④ lives in South Korea

(3) What does the Japanese boy need to do to become a good esports player? ☐
  ① Be strong and healthy.
  ② Spend much time playing computer games.
  ③ Study Korean very hard.
  ④ Talk his parents into letting him become an esports player.

Vocabulary & Grammar 重要表現や文法事項について理解しよう【知識】 (英検®) (GTEC®)

Make the correct choice to complete each sentence. （各3点）

(1) That movie was a complete (　　　) of time.
　　① addict　　　　　② disaster　　　　　③ honor　　　　　④ waste

(2) The mayor's (　　　) leadership eased fears of the citizens during the crisis.
　　① small　　　　　② solid　　　　　③ strong　　　　　④ weak

(3) The restaurant needs to (　　　) its service.
　　① discover　　　　② improve　　　　　③ remember　　　　④ respond

(4) Life isn't always (　　　).
　　① common　　　　② fair　　　　　　③ strong　　　　　④ wide

(5) My grandfather (　　　) me to be an artist.
　　① demands　　　　② hopes　　　　　③ suggests　　　　④ wants

Listening 英文を聞いて理解しよう【知識・技能】【思考力・判断力・表現力】 (共通テスト) ● 24

Listen to the English and make the best choice to match the content. （4点）
　① The speaker is studying English hard to go abroad.
　② The speaker is working hard to become a professional esports player.
　③ The speaker wants to become an English teacher in the future.

Interaction 英文を聞いて会話を続けよう【知識・技能】【思考力・判断力・表現力】 スピーキング・トレーナー ● 25

Listen to the English and respond to the last remark. （7点）
〔メ モ　　　　　　　　　　　　　　　　　　　　　　　　　　　　　　　　　　　　　　　〕

🎧 **Hints**
I want to ～で始めて，将来の夢や目標などを話しましょう。

Production (Speaking) 自分の考えを話して伝えよう【思考力・判断力・表現力】 スピーキング・トレーナー

Answer the following question. （9点）

Do you think esports should become an official Olympic sport? Why?
〔メ モ　　　　　　　　　　　　　　　　　　　　　　　　　　　　　　　　　　　　　　　〕

🎧 **Hints**
eスポーツをオリンピックの正式種目とするべきかどうかについて，自分の考えとその理由を話しましょう。

Mansai, *Kyogen* Performer

Kumi: Look at this poster, / Vivian. //

Vivian: Hmm … // The man / wearing a mask / is dancing, / and the two men are playing music. //

Kumi: Yeah. // This poster was for a *Kyogen* performance / in France. //

5 *Vivian:* I see. // Then, / who are Mansaku, / Mansai, / and Yuki Nomura? //

Kumi: They are famous *Kyogen* performers. // Actually, / they are a grandfather, / a father, / and a son. //

Vivian: Do you think / I'll like watching *Kyogen*? // The stories **seem** difficult / for me. //

10 *Kumi:* Don't worry! // The stories are simple and funny. // In addition, / *Kyogen* has a traditional and beautiful style, / just like *No*, / *Kabuki*, / and *Bunraku*. //

Vivian: Okay. // Now, / I want / to learn more / about *Kyogen*. //

Kumi: **Awesome**! // Let's go / to the theater / **sometime**. //

Vivian: I can't wait! //

(110 words)

🔊 **音読しよう** 📖 ～～～～～～～～～～～　スピーキング・トレーナー

Practice 1 スラッシュ位置で文を区切って読んでみよう ☐

Practice 2 イントネーションに注意して読んでみよう ☐

TRY! 1分15秒以内に本文全体を音読しよう ☐

📖 Reading　本文の内容を読んで理解しよう【知識・技能】【思考力・判断力・表現力】　　(共通テスト)

Make the correct choice to complete each sentence or answer each question. (各5点)

(1) Kumi thinks the stories are ☐ for Vivian to enjoy watching *Kyogen*.

　① boring and difficult enough　　② simple and funny enough

　③ too boring and difficult　　④ too simple and funny

(2) From the dialogue, you have learned that Vivian ☐.

　① is looking forward to going to the theater to watch *Kyogen* with Kumi

　② knew who Mansaku, Mansai, and Yuki Nomura were

　③ wants to learn more about *Kyogen* because she wants to be a performer

　④ wasn't able to wait for Kumi because she wanted to watch *Kyogen* as soon as possible

(3) How will you reply to Vivian's last remark? ☐

　① I can't wait to see you.

　② I don't have enough time, sorry.

　③ We had a good time at the theater.

　④ Why don't we go to see a performance next weekend?

Vocabulary & Grammar　重要表現や文法事項について理解しよう【知識】　英検® GTEC®

Make the correct choice to complete each sentence.　（各3点）

(1) A thin person (　　　) taller than he really is.
　① fails　　　② sees　　　③ seems　　　④ tastes

(2) Do you have any books on this country's (　　　) arts?
　① additional　　② conditional　　③ natural　　④ traditional

(3) He always (　　　) a red T-shirt.
　① puts　　　② suits　　　③ wears　　　④ works

(4) She can speak English and Spanish. (　　　), she says she can understand a little Japanese.
　① For all　　② In addition　　③ In addition to　　④ In spite of

(5) A ship (　　　) more than 5,000 passengers is missing in the Atlantic Ocean.
　① carried　　② carries　　③ carry　　④ carrying

🎧 Listening　英文を聞いて理解しよう【知識・技能】【思考力・判断力・表現力】　共通テスト 💿26

Listen to the English and make the best choice to match the content.　（4点）
　① The speaker had no chance to watch *Kyogen*.
　② The speaker knows nothing about *Kyogen*.
　③ The speaker wants to watch *Kyogen*.

💬 Interaction　英文を聞いて会話を続けよう【知識・技能】【思考力・判断力・表現力】　スピーキング・トレーナー 💿27

Listen to the English and respond to the last remark.　（7点）
〔メモ　　　　　　　　　　　　　　　　　　　　　　　　　　　　　　　　〕

🎧 Hints
文化祭で狂言を演じようという提案に対して，自分の考えを伝えましょう。

✍️ Production (Writing)　自分の考えを書いて伝えよう【思考力・判断力・表現力】

Write your answer to the following question.　（9点）
Do you want to watch *Kyogen* in the theater?　Why?

🎧 Hints
I want [don't want] to ~ because ... の表現を使って書きましょう。

Mansai, *Kyogen* Performer

Mansai was born / in 1966. //   His family has performed *Kyogen* / since the Edo period. //   Both his father and grandfather / are **living** national treasures. // Mansai performed / on stage / for the first time / at the age of three. //

Kyogen is a traditional art / passed down / from one **generation** to another. // 5 *Kyogen* performers go through **severe** training / to learn the tradition. // However, / just being strict / in traditional ways / may not make *Kyogen* better. //

Mansai believes / he can perform *Kyogen* better / by doing different things. // For example, / he studied Shakespeare's plays / in London / in 1994. //   He also acts / in movies / and appears / on TV. //   He even **advised** Yuzuru Hanyu / on 10 his skating program, / *SEIMEI*. //   In this way, / Mansai has drawn people's attention / to *Kyogen*. //

(120 words)

Practice 1　スラッシュ位置で文を区切って読んでみよう ☐
Practice 2　イントネーションに注意して読んでみよう ☐
TRY!　1分25秒以内に本文全体を音読しよう ☐

スピーキング・トレーナー

Reading 本文の内容を読んで理解しよう【知識・技能】【思考力・判断力・表現力】   共通テスト GTEC®

Make the correct choice to complete each sentence or answer each question. （各5点）

(1) What does "severe" mean in line 5? ☐
　　① calm　　　　　② easy　　　　　③ kind　　　　　④ strict

(2) Mansai studied Shakespeare's plays in London because he thought that ☐.
　　① he could perform *Kyogen* better by doing different things
　　② *Kyogen* looked like Shakespeare's plays in many ways
　　③ Shakespeare's plays seemed to be more strict than *Kyogen*
　　④ the style of *Kyogen* should not be changed forever

(3) Which of the following is true? ☐
　　① Both Mansai and his father are living national treasures.
　　② Mansai performed on stage for the first time when he was thirteen.
　　③ Mansai's family has performed *Kyogen* since the Edo period.
　　④ Mansai's father even advised Yuzuru Hanyu on his skating program.

🔖 Vocabulary & Grammar　重要表現や文法事項について理解しよう【知識】　(英検®) (GTEC®)

Make the correct choice to complete each sentence. （各3点）

(1) Japanese people have played *Go* (　　　) the Nara period.

　① for　　　　　② in　　　　　③ on　　　　　④ since

(2) Frogs live (　　　) in water and on land.

　① both　　　　② either　　　　③ neither　　　④ or

(3) I'd like to (　　　) your attention to this novel.

　① draw　　　　② picture　　　　③ pull　　　　④ take

(4) The doctor (　　　) him to stop working too much.

　① advised　　② avoided　　　③ seemed　　　④ suggested

(5) Miso soup is the traditional soup (　　　) at breakfast in Japan.

　① ate　　　　② eaten　　　　③ eating　　　④ eats

🎧 Listening　英文を聞いて理解しよう【知識・技能】【思考力・判断力・表現力】　(共通テスト) (○28)

Listen to the English and make the best choice to match the content. （4点）

　① *Kyogen* is a comedy about interesting events people often experience in their daily lives.

　② *Kyogen* is a tragedy concerning frightening accidents.

　③ The speaker often encounters interesting happenings in her daily life.

💬 Interaction　英文を聞いて会話を続けよう【知識・技能】【思考力・判断力・表現力】　(スピーキング・トレーナー) (○29)

Listen to the English and respond to the last remark. （7点）

　〔メ モ　　　　　　　　　　　　　　　　　　　　　　　　　　　　　　　　　〕

🎧 **Hints**

　I have been ～ing の表現を使って子どものころから続けていることを話しましょう。

💬 Production (Speaking)　自分の考えを話して伝えよう【思考力・判断力・表現力】　(スピーキング・トレーナー)

Answer the following question. （9点）

If you were Mansai, what would you do to draw people's attention to *Kyogen*?

　〔メ モ　　　　　　　　　　　　　　　　　　　　　　　　　　　　　　　　　〕

🎧 **Hints**

　野村萬斎さんの立場になって考えましょう。

One of Mansai's new efforts / **involved digital** technology. // He performed / as a **motion capture** actor / for the movie / *Shin Godzilla* / in 2016. // It was easy / for Mansai / to play the role / of Godzilla. // He moved / in the *Kyogen* style! // "I'm glad / that *Kyogen*'s history / of more than 650 years / is mixed / with the

5 DNA / of Godzilla," / Mansai said. //

Mansai was chosen / as the **adviser** / of the opening and closing ceremonies / of the Tokyo Olympics and Paralympics. // This was / because he worked / on the **fusion** / of **classical** art and **modern** theater. // Mansai's goal is / to become a bridge / to pass on the traditional art / to the next generation. //

(107 words)

Practice 1 スラッシュ位置で文を区切って読んでみよう ☐
Practice 2 イントネーションに注意して読んでみよう ☐
TRY! 1分15秒以内に本文全体を音読しよう ☐

スピーキング・トレーナー

📖 Reading 本文の内容を読んで理解しよう【知識・技能】【思考力・判断力・表現力】 共通テスト GTEC®

Make the correct choice to complete each sentence or answer each question. (各5点)

(1) It was easy for Mansai to play the role of Godzilla because ☐.

① he acted in the way of *Kyogen*

② he was an expert in digital technology

③ he was chosen as the adviser of the opening and closing ceremonies of the Tokyo Olympics and Paralympics

④ he worked on the fusion of classical art and modern theater

(2) You have learned that Mansai ☐.

① taught a motion capture actor how to move in the *Kyogen* style

② wanted to play the role of Godzilla

③ was chosen as the adviser of the movie *Shin Godzilla*

④ was glad that *Kyogen*'s history was mixed with the DNA of Godzilla

(3) What does "fusion" mean in line 8? ☐

① contrast   ② division   ③ mixture   ④ separation

Vocabulary & Grammar　重要表現や文法事項について理解しよう【知識】　英検® GTEC®

Make the correct choice to complete each sentence.　（各3点）

(1) Bill lifted that big box easily, without using much (　　　).

① access ② effort ③ health ④ work

(2) If you (　　　) blue and yellow, you will get green.

① collect ② involve ③ mix ④ treat

(3) The director chose David (　　　) the leading actor.

① as ② on ③ to ④ with

(4) Some people like (　　　) music, while others like pop music.

① classic ② classical ③ classically ④ classic's

(5) (　　　) is natural to smile when you are happy.

① It ② That ③ This ④ What

Listening　英文を聞いて理解しよう【知識・技能】【思考力・判断力・表現力】　共通テスト 🔘30

Listen to the English and make the best choice to match the content.　（4点）

① The speaker has never watched the movie *Shin Godzilla*.

② The speaker likes the movie *Shin Godzilla* the best.

③ The speaker often goes to the movies.

Interaction　英文を聞いて会話を続けよう【知識・技能】【思考力・判断力・表現力】　スピーキング・トレーナー 🔘31

Listen to the English and respond to the last remark.　（7点）

〔メ モ　　　　　　　　　　　　　　　　　　　　　　　　　　　　　　　　　〕

🔑 **Hints**
　I want to ～のように文の形ではなく，伝統文化名だけを答えても構いません。

Production (Writing)　自分の考えを書いて伝えよう【思考力・判断力・表現力】

Write your answer to the following question.　（9点）

Which do you like the best, *Kyogen*, *No*, *Kabuki*, or *Bunraku*? Why?

🔑 **Hints**
　4つの中から一番好きな伝統芸能を選び，ほかとの違いや魅力に言及しながら答えましょう。

In this Corner of the World

A lot of people helped / to make the movie / *In this Corner of the World*. //
When the movie project started, / there was not enough money. //
The **production staff** asked people / to **donate** money / on the Internet. //
Surprisingly, / the staff gathered about 40 million yen / from more than 3,000
5 people. //

The movie became a hit. // One of the reasons / for this / was the power / of
social media. // Good reviews spread, / and more and more people went / to see
it. //

Another reason was / that the movie shows the real life / of a family / during
10 World War II. // The family members led quite an **ordinary** life, / just as we do. //
That **appealed** strongly / to a lot of people. // Ever since the movie came out, /
it has been **attracting** many **viewers**. //

(127 words)

音読しよう　　　　　　　　　　　　　　　　　　　　　　スピーキング・トレーナー

Practice 1　スラッシュ位置で文を区切って読んでみよう ☐
Practice 2　イントネーションに注意して読んでみよう ☐
TRY!　1分30秒以内に本文全体を音読しよう ☐

Reading　本文の内容を読んで理解しよう【知識・技能】【思考力・判断力・表現力】　　　　共通テスト GTEC®

Make the correct choice to complete each sentence or answer each question.　(各5点)

(1) The movie became a hit because ☐.
　① it showed the real life of a family during World War II
　② it showed the unreal life of a family during World War II
　③ the production staff asked people to donate money on the Internet
　④ the production staff donated their money to make it

(2) Which of the following is true?　☐
　① Good reviews of the movie made more and more people go to see the movie.
　② Thanks to donations, the movie became a hit.
　③ The family members in the movie led a hard life.
　④ When the movie project started, there was no money.

(3) What does "ordinary" mean in line 10?　☐
　① different　　　　② original　　　　③ special　　　　④ normal

Goals

🔊 イントネーションを理解して音読することができる。　📖『この世界の片隅に』に関する英文を読んで概要や要点をとらえることができる。
文脈を理解して適切な語句を用いて英文を完成することができる。　🎧 平易な英語で話される短い英文を聞いて必要な情報を聞き取ることができる。
映画について簡単な語句を用いて情報や考えを伝えることができる。　映画について簡単な語句を用いて考えを表現することができる。

✏️ Vocabulary & Grammar　重要表現や文法事項について理解しよう【知識】　　英検® GTEC®

Make the correct choice to complete each sentence. （各3点）

(1) These kinds of movies (　　　　) large crowds.

　　① attract　　　　　② deny　　　　　　③ discover　　　　　④ pull

(2) The event producer says, "We will (　　　　) all profits to charity."

　　① destroy　　　　　② donate　　　　　③ spread　　　　　④ supply

(3) About fifty thousand people visited the new theme park (　　　　) the weekend.

　　① between　　　　　② during　　　　　③ in　　　　　　　④ while

(4) The police (　　　　) the public for information about the crime.

　　① are appealing　　② are appealing to　③ is appealing　　④ is appealing to

(5) I (　　　　) my homework all evening, but I still have a lot more to do.

　　① did　　　　　　　② do　　　　　　　③ have been doing　④ am doing

🎧 Listening　英文を聞いて理解しよう【知識・技能】【思考力・判断力・表現力】　　共通テスト 💿 32

Listen to the English and make the best choice to match the content. （4点）

　　① The speaker is going to participate in the international film festival.

　　② The speaker is interested in international film festivals.

　　③ The speaker knows about international film festivals.

💬 Interaction　英文を聞いて会話を続けよう【知識・技能】【思考力・判断力・表現力】　スピーキング・トレーナー 💿 33

Listen to the English and respond to the last remark. （7点）

　〔メ　モ　　　　　　　　　　　　　　　　　　　　　　　　　　　　　　　　　　　　〕

👆 **Hints**
　My favorite movie is ... や I like ... で始めて，好きな映画を答えましょう。

😀 Production (Speaking)　自分の考えを話して伝えよう【思考力・判断力・表現力】　スピーキング・トレーナー

Answer the following question. （9点）

Which do you like better, live-action movies or animated movies? Why?

　〔メ　モ　　　　　　　　　　　　　　　　　　　　　　　　　　　　　　　　　　　　〕

👆 **Hints**
　実写映画とアニメ映画のそれぞれの特徴を考えましょう。

In this Corner of the World

The main character Suzu / gets **married** / to Shusaku / and moves / from Hiroshima / to Kure. // She tries hard / to get used to the new environment. //

As time passes, / people are running short of food. // Suzu cooks meals / by using wild plants. // One day, / when she cooks, / she uses a **method** / that was
5 **invented** / by a famous samurai / and increases the **amount** / of food. //

Suzu likes drawing pictures. // One day, / when she draws a picture / of **battleships** / on a hill, / the **military** police **suspect** her / of spying. // They **search** her house / for some signs / of spying. // The people / in her family / try hard / not to laugh / because Suzu is so **absent-minded** / that she can never spy! //
10 They **burst** into **laughter** / after the police leave. //

(122 words)

スピーキング・トレーナー

Practice 1 スラッシュ位置で文を区切って読んでみよう ☐
Practice 2 イントネーションに注意して読んでみよう ☐
TRY! 1分25秒以内に本文全体を音読しよう ☐

Reading 本文の内容を読んで理解しよう【知識・技能】【思考力・判断力・表現力】   (共通テスト)

Make the correct choice to complete each sentence or answer each question.

(各5点[(1)と(3)は完答])

(1) Put the following events (①～④) into the order in which they happened.

☐ → ☐ → ☐ → ☐

① Shusaku got married to Suzu.　　② Suzu drew a picture of battleships.
③ Suzu lived in Hiroshima City.　　④ The military police came to Suzu's house.

(2) The military police suspected Suzu of spying because ☐.
① she burst into laughter in front of the police
② she cooked meals by using wild plants
③ she drew a picture of battleships
④ she got married to Shusaku

(3) According to the article you read, which of the following are true? (Choose two options. The order does not matter.) ☐ · ☐
① Suzu got married to Shusaku and moved from Hiroshima to Kure.
② After the police left, the people in Suzu's family burst into laughter.
③ The military police found some signs of spying in Suzu's house.
④ The military police searched for a method that was invented by a famous samurai.
⑤ Though people were running short of food, they didn't know what to do.

🔖 Vocabulary & Grammar　重要表現や文法事項について理解しよう【知識】　英検® GTEC®

Make the correct choice to complete each sentence.　（各3点）

(1) The reason Betty (　　　　) Jack was that he was attractive and intelligent.
　① is married　　　② married　　　③ married to　　　④ married with

(2) When I was living in the country, I (　　　　) up early in the morning.
　① got used to get　② got used to got　③ was used to get　④ was used to getting

(3) We'd better stop at the next gas station to fill up because we are (　　　） gas.
　① run short　　　② run short of　　　③ running short　　　④ running short of

(4) The police are (　　　） the woods for the missing girl.
　① developing　　② finding　　　③ inventing　　　④ searching

(5) I met a man (　　　） I thought was an actor.
　① what　　　　② which　　　　③ who　　　　④ whose

🎧 Listening　英文を聞いて理解しよう【知識・技能】【思考力・判断力・表現力】　共通テスト　🔘34

Listen to the English and make the best choice to match the content.　（4点）

　① During World War II, people felt very anxious.
　② During World War II, people had nothing to eat.
　③ During World War II, people tried hard to cook meals.

💬 Interaction　英文を聞いて会話を続けよう【知識・技能】【思考力・判断力・表現力】　スピーキング・トレーナー　🔘35

Listen to the English and respond to the last remark.　（7点）

〔メモ　　　　　　　　　　　　　　　　　　　　　　　　　　　　　　　　　　　　〕

🖐 **Hints**
I recommend ... で始めて，おすすめの映画を紹介しましょう。

✍ Production（Writing）　自分の考えを書いて伝えよう【思考力・判断力・表現力】

Write your answer to the following question.　（9点）

What is the best animated movie that you have ever seen？　Why？

🖐 **Hints**
一番好きなアニメ映画を取り上げ，好きな理由も含めて説明しましょう。

Shusaku asks Suzu / to come / to his office / with a notebook / which he forgot. //
*Actually, / he wants / to talk / with her. // On a bridge, / they are having a **chat** /*
*about their **fateful** meeting / and married life. //*

Suzu: I guess / I'm just afraid / I'll wake up / from a dream. //

5 *Shusaku:* Dream? //

Suzu: Having to change my name / and move **somewhere** new / was hard /
for me, / but you've been so kind, / and I've made friends. // I don't want / to
wake up / because I'm really happy / to be who I am today. //

Shusaku: I see. // The past and the **paths** / we did not choose, / I guess, / are

10 really like a dream, / if you think / about it. // Suzu, / choosing to marry you /
was the best decision / of my life. //

(121 words)

Practice 1 スラッシュ位置で文を区切って読んでみよう ☐
Practice 2 イントネーションに注意して読んでみよう ☐
TRY! 1分25秒以内に本文全体を音読しよう ☐

📖 Reading 本文の内容を読んで理解しよう【知識・技能】【思考力・判断力・表現力】 (共通テスト) (GTEC®)

Make the correct choice to complete each sentence or answer each question. (各5点)

(1) Shusaku asked Suzu to bring a notebook to his office because ☐.
　① he wanted her to wake him up
　② he wanted to marry her
　③ he wanted to talk with her
　④ he wanted to use it

(2) What does "guess" mean in line 4? ☐
　① expect　　　　② feel　　　　③ suppose　　　　④ tell

(3) Which of the following is true? ☐
　① It was easy for Suzu to change her name and move somewhere new.
　② Shusaku asked Suzu to buy a new notebook because he lost his notebook.
　③ Shusaku thought it was right that he made up his mind to marry Suzu.
　④ Suzu wanted to wake up from a dream because she wasn't happy.

🏷 Vocabulary & Grammar　重要表現や文法事項について理解しよう【知識】　英検® GTEC®

Make the correct choice to complete each sentence.　（各3点）

(1) Don't (　　　) to mail this letter on your way to school.

① avoid ② decide ③ forget ④ suggest

(2) I (　　　) up two hours earlier than usual, but I couldn't sleep again.

① put ② took ③ went ④ woke

(3) We can't make a (　　　) until we get useful information.

① culture ② decision ③ division ④ feature

(4) At that time I looked back on my (　　　).

① billion ② fuel ③ past ④ population

(5) This is a picture (　　　) she sent me the other day.

① what ② which ③ who ④ whose

🎧 Listening　英文を聞いて理解しよう【知識・技能】【思考力・判断力・表現力】　共通テスト　💿 36

Listen to the English and make the best choice to match the content.　（4点）

① The speaker has seen movies about World War II.

② The speaker lived an ordinary life during World War II.

③ The speaker wants to learn about World War II.

💬 Interaction　英文を聞いて会話を続けよう【知識・技能】【思考力・判断力・表現力】　スピーキング・トレーナー　💿 37

Listen to the English and respond to the last remark.　（7点）

〔メモ　　　　　　　　　　　　　　　　　　　　　　　　　　　　　〕

🔑 **Hints**
A-bomb Dome (原爆ドーム), Hiroshima Peace Memorial Museum (広島平和記念資料館), Children's Peace Monument (原爆の子の像)

✍ Production (Writing)　自分の考えを書いて伝えよう【思考力・判断力・表現力】

Write your answer to the following question.　（9点）

Are you happy with your current life?　Why?

....

....

🔑 **Hints**
I am (not) happy with ... や I am (not) satisfied with ... などの表現を使って書きましょう。

In this Corner of the World

Gradually, / the situation gets worse. // Suzu and her **niece** / experience an air **raid.** // When they are walking / hand in hand / after the raid, / an **unexploded** bomb **explodes.** // Her niece is killed / and Suzu loses her right hand. //

About four months after the war ends, / Suzu finds / "the new bomb" has
5 taken the lives / of her mother and father. // Her younger sister / is **ill** in bed. // She has lost people / she loves. //

Through the movie, / we can find out / how people lived / during the war. // They led ordinary lives. // They shared time / with their families. // Sometimes / they laughed together, / and sometimes / they cried together. // Our lives today /
10 are the same / as theirs were. // The movie shows / that such ordinary lives / are really precious. //

(122 words)

音読しよう

スピーキング・トレーナー

Practice 1 スラッシュ位置で文を区切って読んでみよう ☐
Practice 2 イントネーションに注意して読んでみよう ☐
TRY! 1分25秒以内に本文全体を音読しよう ☐

📖 Reading 本文の内容を読んで理解しよう【知識・技能】【思考力・判断力・表現力】 共通テスト

Make the correct choice to complete each sentence or answer each question. （各5点）

(1) Who lost their right hand when the bomb exploded? ☐
　① Suzu　　　　　　　　　　② Suzu's mother and father
　③ Suzu's niece　　　　　　 ④ Suzu's younger sister

(2) About four months after the war ended, Suzu found that ☐.
　① her mother and father died
　② her niece lost her right hand
　③ her younger brother was ill in bed
　④ she lost her right hand

(3) What will you find out if you watch the movie? ☐
　① The differences between life during the war and our life today.
　② The reason why people cried together.
　③ The way people lived before the war.
　④ The way people shared time with their families during the war.

🏷 Vocabulary & Grammar 重要表現や文法事項について理解しよう【知識】 (英検®) (GTEC®)

Make the correct choice to complete each sentence. （各3点）

(1) Mike has been ill (　　　) bed for a week.

① at ② in ③ into ④ on

(2) The army will carry out a (　　　) with 20 men.

① donation ② mistake ③ raid ④ weapon

(3) I (　　　) out how to say "hello" in Japanese.

① found ② looked ③ pulled ④ searched

(4) Our patient is in the (　　　) condition as yesterday.

① correct ② different ③ difficult ④ same

(5) Excuse me. Do you know (　　　)?

① what is the museum ② when the museum is

③ where is the museum ④ where the museum is

🎧 Listening 英文を聞いて理解しよう【知識・技能】【思考力・判断力・表現力】 (共通テスト) 💿 38

Listen to the English and make the best choice to match the content. （4点）

① Hiroshima was damaged by the atomic bomb.

② Many people have suffered from the atomic bomb.

③ World War II started on August 6, 1945.

💬 Interaction 英文を聞いて会話を続けよう【知識・技能】【思考力・判断力・表現力】 (スピーキング・トレーナー) 💿 39

Listen to the English and respond to the last remark. （7点）

〔メモ 　　　　　　　　　　　　　　　　　　　　　　　　　　　　　　　　　　　　　〕

🔑 **Hints**
姪を亡くしたときのすずの気持ちを想像してみましょう。

✍ Production (Writing) 自分の考えを書いて伝えよう【思考力・判断力・表現力】

Write your answer to the following question. （9点）

What do you think is important to achieve world peace?

🔑 **Hints**
世界平和を実現するために，身近にできることを考えましょう。

Should Stores Stay Open for 24 Hours?

There are a lot of stores and restaurants / around us. // We take it for **granted** / that some of them are open / for 24 hours. // This business model has been popular. // It has brought us some **advantages**. //

First, / our lives have become convenient. // At a convenience store, / we can
5 buy things, / pay **bills**, / and mail packages / at any time. // People / who work late at night / can eat / at a 24-hour restaurant / before or after work. //

Second, / our lives have become safer / thanks to 24-hour stores and restaurants. // People in danger / can ask for help / there. // **Analysts** tell us / that convenience stores play the role / of *koban*, / or police boxes, / especially at
10 night. //

(111 words)

🔊)) 音読しよう 📖 ──────────────── スピーキング・トレーナー

Practice 1 スラッシュ位置で文を区切って読んでみよう ☐
Practice 2 英語の音の変化に注意して読んでみよう ☐
TRY! 1分10秒以内に本文全体を音読しよう ☐

📖 Reading 本文の内容を読んで理解しよう【知識・技能】【思考力・判断力・表現力】 (共通テスト)

Make the correct choice to complete each sentence or answer each question. (各5点)

(1) Thanks to the convenience stores around us, we can ☐.
　① ask the way without going to a police box
　② buy things, eat meals, and take a rest
　③ mail packages without going to a post office
　④ pay bills, use a bathroom, and go to sleep

(2) You have learned that 24-hour stores and restaurants ☐.
　① have made our lives convenient
　② have made our lives inconvenient
　③ have made our lives more dangerous
　④ have so many disadvantages for us

(3) Which is the best title for the article? ☐
　① How Have 24-hour Stores Become Popular?
　② The Advantages of 24-hour Stores and Restaurants
　③ The Disadvantages of 24-hour Stores and Restaurants
　④ What Can We Do at Convenience Stores?

🏷 Vocabulary & Grammar　重要表現や文法事項について理解しよう【知識】　英検® GTEC®

Make the correct choice to complete each sentence.　(各3点)

(1) I took it (　　　) granted that you were acquainted with the facts.

① as　　　　② for　　　　③ to　　　　④ with

(2) His experience gave him a big (　　　) in his new business.

① advantage　　② information　　③ package　　④ technology

(3) Today, (　　　) the Internet, we can get a lot of information easily.

① as well　　② for all　　③ in spite of　　④ thanks to

(4) If you want to leave a classroom early, you should (　　　) permission.

① ask for　　② hear of　　③ listen to　　④ talk about

(5) Alice (　　　) she wanted to quit our company.

① said me that　　② spoke me that　　③ told me that　　④ told to me that

🎧 Listening　英文を聞いて理解しよう【知識・技能】【思考力・判断力・表現力】　共通テスト 🔘40

Listen to the English and make the best choice to match the content.　(4点)

① The speaker is against the construction of the new convenience store.

② The speaker is happy with the new convenience store.

③ The speaker often goes to the new convenience store.

💬 Interaction　英文を聞いて会話を続けよう【知識・技能】【思考力・判断力・表現力】　スピーキング・トレーナー 🔘41

Listen to the English and respond to the last remark.　(7点)

〔メモ　　　　　　　　　　　　　　　　　　　　　　　　　　　〕

Hints

inconvenient (不便な)，unhappy (悲しい，不満な) などの表現を使って話しましょう。

😀 Production (Speaking)　自分の考えを話して伝えよう【思考力・判断力・表現力】　スピーキング・トレーナー

Answer the following question.　(9点)

How often do you go to a convenience store?　And what for?

〔メモ　　　　　　　　　　　　　　　　　　　　　　　　　　　〕

Hints

コンビニを利用する目的については，本文第2段落の内容も参考にして答えましょう。

Convenience stores started / with an ice shop / in the U.S. / in the 1920s. // Later, / the ice shop started / to sell daily **necessities** and food / as well. // In the 1970s, / this idea came to Japan. // **Unlike** convenience stores now, / stores at that time / were only open / from early in the morning / till late at night. //

5   Until the 1970s, / there were almost no stores or restaurants / open at night / in Japan. // Many Japanese people / at that time / worked / during the day / and stayed home / at night. //

The Japanese **economy** developed **rapidly**, / especially in the early 1970s. // There was social **demand** / for people / to work / at night. // The change / in 10   people's working styles / **allowed around-the-clock** stores / to appear / in Japan. // Now, / 24-hour convenience stores / can be seen everywhere. //

(125 words)

音読しよう

Practice 1 スラッシュ位置で文を区切って読んでみよう ☐
Practice 2 英語の音の変化に注意して読んでみよう ☐
TRY! 1分20秒以内に本文全体を音読しよう ☐

スピーキング・トレーナー

Reading 本文の内容を読んで理解しよう【知識・技能】【思考力・判断力・表現力】   共通テスト GTEC®

Make the correct choice to complete each sentence or answer each question. （各5点）

(1) The rapid development of the Japanese economy in the early 1970s ☐.
   ① made convenience stores start to open till late at night
   ② made people work during the day
   ③ made people work from early in the morning till late at night
   ④ made stores start to open for 24 hours

(2) Which of the following is true? ☐
   ① Convenience stores started with an ice shop in Japan in the 1920s.
   ② Stores used to open only from early in the morning till late at night.
   ③ Today, around-the-clock convenience stores cannot be seen everywhere in Japan.
   ④ Until the 1970s, there were almost no stores open at night in the U.S.

(3) What does "demand" mean in line 9? ☐
   ① answer   ② need   ③ offer   ④ work

Vocabulary & Grammar　重要表現や文法事項について理解しよう【知識】　英検® GTEC®

Make the correct choice to complete each sentence.　(各3点)

(1) (　　　) her sisters, Nancy has no talent for music.

　① Besides　　　　② Opposite　　　　③ Unlike　　　　④ Within

(2) There are signs of recovery in the (　　　).

　① economic　　　② economical　　　③ economist　　　④ economy

(3) We (　　　) our son to use the family car.

　① allowed　　　　② let　　　　③ made　　　　④ suggested

(4) I did well on the English listening test because I understood (　　　) on the CD.

　① almost everything ② almost nothing　　③ even anything　　④ only nothing

(5) The medicine should be (　　　) three times a day.

　① eaten　　　　② eating　　　　③ taken　　　　④ taking

🎧 Listening　英文を聞いて理解しよう【知識・技能】【思考力・判断力・表現力】　共通テスト 💿42

Listen to the English and make the best choice to match the content.　(4点)

　① The speaker has been to China.

　② There are so many convenience stores in Japan.

　③ We cannot find any convenience stores overseas.

💬 Interaction　英文を聞いて会話を続けよう【知識・技能】【思考力・判断力・表現力】　スピーキング・トレーナー 💿43

Listen to the English and respond to the last remark.　(7点)

〔メ モ　　　　　　　　　　　　　　　　　　　　　　　　　　　　　　　　　〕

🎧 **Hints**
Yes か No だけではなく，その理由も含めて話しましょう。

✍ Production (Writing)　自分の考えを書いて伝えよう【思考力・判断力・表現力】

Write your answer to the following question.　(9点)

When you need to buy something, do you usually go to a supermarket or a convenience store? Why?

🎧 **Hints**
スーパーとコンビニのどちらをよく利用するかについて書きましょう。

Should Stores Stay Open for 24 Hours?

Part 3

教科書 p.100-101 　/ 50

It is true / that 24-hour stores have some advantages, / but they also have **disadvantages**. // For example, / they **contribute** to environmental problems. // Opening stores / for 24 hours / **requires** a lot of energy / and **emits** CO_2. // In addition, / stores throw away much **unsold** food. //

5 　A **labor shortage** / is another problem. // Due to the falling **birthrate** / and aging **population**, / the number of people / who can work / late at night / has been **decreasing**. // Owners of convenience stores think / that it is difficult / to **employ** enough staff members. //

Should stores stay open / for 24 hours? // It is time / to think / about what

10 our society really needs. // Some stores have stopped / opening for 24 hours. // Time will tell. //

(112 words)

🔊)) 音読しよう 📖 ⌇⌇⌇⌇⌇⌇⌇⌇⌇⌇⌇⌇⌇⌇⌇⌇⌇⌇⌇⌇⌇⌇ スピーキング・トレーナー

Practice 1 スラッシュ位置で文を区切って読んでみよう ☐
Practice 2 英語の音の変化に注意して読んでみよう ☐
TRY! 1分10秒以内に本文全体を音読しよう ☐

📖 Reading 本文の内容を読んで理解しよう【知識・技能】【思考力・判断力・表現力】 　共通テスト GTEC®

Make the correct choice to complete each sentence or answer each question. (各5点)

(1) What does "emit" mean in line 3? ☐
　　① give in 　　　　② give off 　　　　③ take in 　　　　④ take off

(2) It is true that opening stores for 24 hours has ☐.
　　① both environmental problems and a labor shortage problem
　　② neither environmental problems nor a labor shortage problem
　　③ only a labor shortage problem
　　④ only environmental problems

(3) Which of the following is **not** true? ☐
　　① It is difficult for owners of convenience stores to hire enough staff members.
　　② It is not so difficult for owners of convenience stores to fire all the staff members.
　　③ Opening stores for 24 hours increases garbage.
　　④ Opening stores for 24 hours needs a lot of energy and emits CO_2.

Vocabulary & Grammar 　重要表現や文法事項について理解しよう【知識】　　英検®　GTEC®

Make the correct choice to complete each sentence. （各3点）

(1) The students (　　　) most of their free time to the clean-up campaign in the local community.

① combined ② contributed ③ divided ④ opposed

(2) In Japan, the law (　　　) every car owner to pay a tax every year.

① realizes ② remembers ③ requires ④ responds

(3) He was absent from class (　　　) a pain in his leg.

① at the cost of ② due to ③ for the purpose of ④ in spite of

(4) (　　　) foreign travelers who visit Japan is very large.

① A number of ② Numbers of ③ The number of ④ The numbers of

(5) (　　　) seems easy at first often turns out to be difficult.

① That ② What ③ Which ④ Who

Listening 　英文を聞いて理解しよう【知識・技能】【思考力・判断力・表現力】　　共通テスト 44

Listen to the English and make the best choice to match the content. （4点）

① Japan has nothing to do with the problem of food waste.

② The speaker has a good idea to solve the problem of food waste.

③ The speaker thinks that we should deal with the problem of food waste.

Interaction 　英文を聞いて会話を続けよう【知識・技能】【思考力・判断力・表現力】　スピーキング・トレーナー 45

Listen to the English and respond to the last remark. （7点）

〔メモ 　　　　　　　　　　　　　　　　　　　　　　　　　　　　　　　　　　〕

🔑 **Hints**
少子高齢化が引き起こす問題について考えましょう。

Production (Speaking) 　自分の考えを話して伝えよう【思考力・判断力・表現力】　スピーキング・トレーナー

Answer the following question. （9点）

What can you do to solve the problem of food waste?

〔メモ 　　　　　　　　　　　　　　　　　　　　　　　　　　　　　　　　　　〕

🔑 **Hints**
食品ロスの問題を解決するために，あなたの身の回りでできることを考えましょう。

David: Do you think / stores should stay open / for 24 hours? //

Taro: Yes. // They're **essential** / for us / in modern society. // I wonder / how people had lived / before convenience stores started. // Thanks to 24-hour stores, / we can buy things / at night. //

5 *David:* I see. // You mean / our lives have become convenient. // How about you, / Kumi? //

Kumi: I don't think / stores should stay open / for 24 hours. // Going shopping / late at night / can be dangerous. // There are a lot of **crimes**, / especially at night. // I really think / we have to find new **lifestyles** / without 24-hour

10   stores. //

David: That's interesting. // We have to change our way / of thinking, / right? // In Europe, / most stores are closed / at night. // I hear / that **self-service** stores will become more **common** / in Japan. //

(120 words)

音読しよう   スピーキング・トレーナー

Practice 1 スラッシュ位置で文を区切って読んでみよう ☐
Practice 2 英語の音の変化に注意して読んでみよう ☐
TRY! 1分15秒以内に本文全体を音読しよう ☐

📖 **Reading** 本文の内容を読んで理解しよう【知識・技能】【思考力・判断力・表現力】   (共通テスト)

Make the correct choice to complete each sentence or answer each question. (各5点)

(1) From Taro's remark, you have learned that Taro thinks ☐.
  ① we can enjoy shopping anywhere in Japan
  ② we can go shopping only at night
  ③ we can live without 24-hour stores
  ④ we cannot live without 24-hour stores

(2) David is interested in Kumi's opinion that ☐.
  ① most stores are closed at night in Europe
  ② people have to find new lifestyles without 24-hour stores
  ③ self-service stores will become more common in Japan
  ④ stores should stay open for 24 hours

(3) Who thinks stores should open for 24 hours? ☐
  ① David   ② Kumi   ③ Taro   ④ Taro and David

🏷️ Vocabulary & Grammar　重要表現や文法事項について理解しよう【知識】　　英検® GTEC®

Make the correct choice to complete each sentence.　（各3点）

(1) I (　　　) why Mary didn't come to the party.

　① insist　　　　② suggest　　　　③ think　　　　④ wonder

(2) It is the job of the police to prevent (　　　).

　① crimes　　　　② directions　　　　③ prisons　　　　④ prizes

(3) Regular exercise is part of a healthy (　　　).

　① habitat　　　　② ingredient　　　　③ lifestyle　　　　④ schedule

(4) Susie and Kate are sisters, but they have nothing at all in (　　　).

　① common　　　　② different　　　　③ same　　　　④ similar

(5) The train (　　　) when I reached the platform, so I didn't have to wait in the cold.

　① arriving　　　　　　　　② arrives

　③ had already arrived　　　④ has already arrived

🎧 Listening　英文を聞いて理解しよう【知識・技能】【思考力・判断力・表現力】　共通テスト　💿 46

Listen to the English and make the best choice to match the content.　（4点）

　① The international student is from England.

　② The speaker is an international student from England.

　③ The speaker is surprised to know that most stores in Japan are open at night.

💬 Interaction　英文を聞いて会話を続けよう【知識・技能】【思考力・判断力・表現力】　スピーキング・トレーナー　💿 47

Listen to the English and respond to the last remark.　（7点）

　〔メ　モ　　　　　　　　　　　　　　　　　　　　　　　　　　　〕

🔑 **Hints**

コンビニにあれば便利だと思うサービスを考えて話しましょう。

✒️ Production（Writing）　自分の考えを書いて伝えよう【思考力・判断力・表現力】

Write your answer to the following question.　（9点）

High school students shouldn't go shopping late at night. What do you think about this?

🔑 **Hints**

自分の考えを支持する理由や具体例を提示しながら意見を伝えましょう。

AI has been an important **issue** / for us. // Some people talk / about the bright future / that AI will bring us. // Others worry / that AI may take away our jobs. // Let's look at the figures below, / and **consider** these differences / in **attitudes** / toward AI. //

5   Figure 1 shows / that 41.8% of people / in their twenties / worry about losing their jobs / due to AI. // On the other hand, / only 19.9% of people / aged over 60 / worry about it. // Younger people feel more **uneasy** / about this **negative** side / of AI. //

Concerning other areas / of AI, / Figure 2 shows / that younger people have
10   more positive attitudes / toward AI. // About 10% of people / in their twenties and thirties / think / AI will have a **favorable impact** / on their lives. // About half this **percentage** / of older people / have positive **images** / of AI. //

(134 words)

🔊)) 音読しよう 📖 ▶   スピーキング・トレーナー

Practice 1 スラッシュ位置で文を区切って読んでみよう ☐
Practice 2 英語の音の変化に注意して読んでみよう ☐
TRY! 1分25秒以内に本文全体を音読しよう ☐

📖 **Reading** 本文の内容を読んで理解しよう【知識・技能】【思考力・判断力・表現力】   共通テスト GTEC®

Make the correct choice to complete each sentence or answer each question. (各5点[(3)は完答])

(1) According to Figure 1, ☐ due to AI.
  ① both younger people and senior citizens worry about losing their jobs
  ② neither younger people nor senior citizens worry about losing their jobs
  ③ only senior citizens worry about losing their jobs
  ④ only younger people worry about losing their jobs

(2) What does "uneasy" mean in line 7? ☐
  ① anxious   ② brave   ③ happy   ④ sad

(3) According to the article and the figures, which of the following are true?
  (Choose two options. The order does not matter.) ☐ · ☐
  ① Around 10% of people in their twenties think AI will have a positive impact on their lives.
  ② More than 50% of people in their twenties worry about losing their jobs due to AI.
  ③ Only about 5% of people in their thirties have positive images of AI.
  ④ Only about 5% of senior citizens have positive images of AI.
  ⑤ Under 20% of people in their thirties worry about losing their jobs due to AI.

🔊 英語の音の変化を理解して音読することができる。　📖 AI に関する英文を読んで概要や要点をとらえることができる。
📝 文脈を理解して適切な語句を用いて英文を完成することができる。　🎧 平易な英語で話される短い英文を聞いて必要な情報を聞き取ることができる。
💬 ロボットについて簡単な語句を用いて情報や考えを伝えることができる。　✍ AI について簡単な語句を用いて考えを表現することができる。

🏷 Vocabulary & Grammar　重要表現や文法事項について理解しよう【知識】　英検® GTEC®

Make the correct choice to complete each sentence.　(各3点)

(1) Have you ever (　　　) majoring in science at university?
　　① considered　　② donated　　③ insisted　　④ learned

(2) Her speech had a great (　　　) on the audience.
　　① attitude　　② confidence　　③ impact　　④ opportunity

(3) When he had a job interview the other day, he made a (　　　) impression on all the interviewers.
　　① favor　　② favorable　　③ favored　　④ favorite

(4) He has a very (　　　) approach to his job.
　　① anxious　　② negative　　③ uneasy　　④ useful

(5) Some like watching *anime*, but (　　　) don't like them.
　　① other　　② others　　③ the other　　④ the others

🎧 Listening　英文を聞いて理解しよう【知識・技能】【思考力・判断力・表現力】　共通テスト 💿 48

Listen to the English and make the best choice to match the content.　(4点)
　　① A smart speaker cannot do various things.
　　② A smart speaker is easily operated by voice.
　　③ The speaker is operating a smart speaker now.

💬 Interaction　英文を聞いて会話を続けよう【知識・技能】【思考力・判断力・表現力】　スピーキング・トレーナー 💿 49

Listen to the English and respond to the last remark.　(7点)
　　〔メ モ　　　　　　　　　　　　　　　　　　　　　　　　　　　　　　　　　　〕

🔖 **Hints**
　I want a robot which ～の表現を使ってどんなロボットがほしいか答えましょう。

✍ Production (Writing)　自分の考えを書いて伝えよう【思考力・判断力・表現力】

Write your answer to the following question.　(9点)
What do you think are the advantages of AI?

🔖 **Hints**
　「Did You Know? ① AI とは？」(教科書 p. 114)の内容も参考にして書きましょう。

We often talk about AI, / but what is it **exactly**? // It is a computer program / which can do a lot of **tasks** / with **accuracy**. // It repeats the tasks, / keeping its accuracy / over a long time. // Even **human-level** AI / can be realized / by deep learning. //

5 Deep learning is a technology / which **enables** a machine / to learn / by itself, / like humans do. // This type of AI / discovers different **features** / in an **object** / and repeats the **process** / until it can **recognize** the object. // As a result, / it can learn / to tell an object from others / with accuracy. //

This technology is used / for **self-driving** cars. // The AI recognizes stop signs /

10 and traffic lights, / so the self-driving cars stop **precisely** / at **intersections**. // Traffic **lane** lines are recognized, / so cars keep / **within** their own lanes. // AI contributes to safe driving. //

(134 words)

 音読しよう ━━━━━━━━━━━━━━━━━━━━━━━ スピーキング・トレーナー

Practice 1 スラッシュ位置で文を区切って読んでみよう ☐
Practice 2 英語の音の変化に注意して読んでみよう ☐
TRY! 1分25秒以内に本文全体を音読しよう ☐

📖 Reading 本文の内容を読んで理解しよう【知識・技能】【思考力・判断力・表現力】　　(共通テスト)

Make the correct choice to complete each sentence or answer each question. (各5点)

(1) Complete your note with the most appropriate item. ☐

　① do lots of tasks accurately

　② make mistakes

　③ organize a computer program

　④ talk about itself

Your Note
AI can:
· ☐ .
· repeat the tasks.
· keep its accuracy over a long time.

(2) Thanks to the technology of deep learning, AI ☐ .

　① can continue discovering different features in an object until it understands the object

　② can learn to find out only the same features in an object

　③ can't continue discovering different features in an object unless it forgets the object

　④ can't learn to find out the different features in an object

(3) You have learned that ☐ .

　① AI can't learn to distinguish an object from others

　② AI is a computer program which can do a lot of tasks with accuracy only for a short time

　③ self-driving cars cannot stop at intersections even if the AI recognizes stop signs and traffic lights

　④ the technology of deep learning enables a machine to learn by itself as humans do

Vocabulary & Grammar　重要表現や文法事項について理解しよう【知識】　英検® GTEC®

Make the correct choice to complete each sentence.　（各3点）

(1) A college education will (　　　) you to get a broader view of the world.
　　① enable　　　　　② let　　　　　　　③ make　　　　　　④ take

(2) Her change was so great that I couldn't (　　　) her.
　　① realize　　　　　② recognize　　　　③ remember　　　　④ remind

(3) It has snowed heavily for a week. (　　　), all the transportation in the city has stopped.
　　① As a result　　　② As far as　　　　③ As long as　　　　④ As to

(4) The building is (　　　) five minutes' walk of the station.
　　① by　　　　　　　② during　　　　　　③ for　　　　　　　④ within

(5) We walked along the shore, (　　　) stones into the sea.
　　① having thrown　② throw　　　　　　③ throwing　　　　　④ thrown

Listening　英文を聞いて理解しよう【知識・技能】【思考力・判断力・表現力】　共通テスト　50

Listen to the English and make the best choice to match the content.　（4点）
　　① The speaker has a self-driving car.
　　② The speaker bought a new self-driving car for her grandfather.
　　③ The speaker's grandfather owns a self-driving car.

Interaction　英文を聞いて会話を続けよう【知識・技能】【思考力・判断力・表現力】　スピーキング・トレーナー　51

Listen to the English and respond to the last remark.　（7点）

〔メモ　　　　　　　　　　　　　　　　　　　　　　　　　　　　　　　　　　　　　　〕

Hints
自動運転車の特徴については，useful (便利な)，high-tech (ハイテクな)，expensive (高価な)などと表すことができます。

Production (Writing)　自分の考えを書いて伝えよう【思考力・判断力・表現力】

Write your answer to the following question.　（9点）
Do you think that elderly drivers should buy a self-driving car?　Why?

Hints
自動運転車のメリット，デメリットを考えて答えましょう。

Our Future with Artificial Intelligence

AI is used / in **facial recognition** technology / at airports. // **Passengers** now often need / to wait / in lines / and show their passports and boarding passes / at gates. // Thanks to this technology, / however, / they won't need / to do these things, / and they can save travel time. //

5　AI is also useful / for **predicting** the times / when crimes are **likely** to happen. // It can predict the places / where crimes will happen, / too. // By using this technology, / police officers can **prevent** crimes / from happening. // As the number of crimes decreases, / society will become safer. //

AI, / however, / has some negative features. // For example, / it is becoming

10　difficult / for even AI engineers / to understand AI's way / of thinking / exactly. // Considering the negative features, / we must try / to use AI carefully. //

(123 words)

🔊))　**音読しよう**　📖　　　　　　　　　　　　　　　　　　スピーキング・トレーナー

Practice 1 スラッシュ位置で文を区切って読んでみよう ☐
Practice 2 英語の音の変化に注意して読んでみよう ☐
TRY! 1分15秒以内に本文全体を音読しよう ☐

📖 Reading　本文の内容を読んで理解しよう【知識・技能】【思考力・判断力・表現力】　　(共通テスト)

Make the correct choice to complete each sentence or answer each question. (各 5 点 [(3)は完答])

(1) Thanks to facial recognition technology, passengers will **not** need to ☐.
　① apply for passports when they go abroad
　② bring their passports when they go abroad
　③ buy boarding passes when they take an airplane
　④ show their boarding passes when they check in

(2) You have learned that police officers ☐ if they use AI.
　① can have strong social connections　　② can prevent crimes from happening
　③ will be able to arrest criminals easily　④ won't be needed anymore

(3) According to the article you read, which of the following are true? (Choose two options. The order does not matter.) ☐ · ☐
　① AI can tell us when and where crimes seem to happen.
　② If the police can prevent crimes from happening, society will become safer.
　③ It is easy for AI engineers to understand AI's way of thinking.
　④ There are no negative features of AI.
　⑤ We don't need to use AI carefully.

🏷 Vocabulary & Grammar　重要表現や文法事項について理解しよう【知識】　英検® GTEC®

Make the correct choice to complete each sentence.　(各3点)

(1)　The airport was crowded with thousands of (　　　) from delayed flights.

　　① clients　　　　② customers　　　　③ guests　　　　④ passengers

(2)　Even scientists cannot (　　　) earthquakes.

　　① announce　　　② debate　　　　③ organize　　　　④ predict

(3)　The heavy snow prevented us (　　　) on time.

　　① from arriving　② in arriving　　③ of arriving　　④ to arriving

(4)　This plan is (　　　) to be a great success.

　　① eager　　　　② free　　　　　③ likely　　　　④ willing

(5)　I believe the day will come (　　　) there will be no war.

　　① that　　　　　② when　　　　　③ where　　　　④ which

🎧 Listening　英文を聞いて理解しよう【知識・技能】【思考力・判断力・表現力】　共通テスト ◎52

Listen to the English and make the best choice to match the content.　(4点)

　　① AI is smarter than human beings.

　　② All researchers agree that AI will be smarter than human beings in the future.

　　③ The day may come when AI will become smarter than human beings.

💬 Interaction　英文を聞いて会話を続けよう【知識・技能】【思考力・判断力・表現力】　スピーキング・トレーナー ◎53

Listen to the English and respond to the last remark.　(7点)

〔メモ　　　　　　　　　　　　　　　　　　　　　　　　　　　　　　　　　〕

🔑 **Hints**

「Did You Know? ② AI の活用事例」（教科書 p. 115）の内容も参考にして話しましょう。

✒ Production (Writing)　自分の考えを書いて伝えよう【思考力・判断力・表現力】

Write your answer to the following question.　(9点)

It may be possible for AI to acquire the same emotions as humans in the near future.
What do you think about this?　And why?

🔑 **Hints**

possible（可能な），impossible（不可能な），emotion（感情），reveal（…を明らかにする）

Our Future with Artificial Intelligence

Local governments are trying / to use AI / to offer better **medical** services / to their **citizens**. // When a small child suddenly gets sick, / young parents often feel uneasy. // There is now an AI system / that can give helpful advice / to uneasy parents. // The way / they use the system / is by entering medical
5 information / into their computers or smartphones. //

The AI system also helps / to **relieve** the **burdens** / of people / working in **emergency** medical services. // Emergency calls come / one after another, / especially after local **clinics** are closed. // The AI system can try / to **cope** with emergency cases / before workers do. //

10 AI will be used / in more fields, / and it will improve our **quality** / of life. // We will be able to live well / with AI / if we can make good use of it. //

(130 words)

スピーキング・トレーナー

🔊)) 音読しよう

Practice 1 スラッシュ位置で文を区切って読んでみよう ☐
Practice 2 英語の音の変化に注意して読んでみよう ☐
TRY! 1分20秒以内に本文全体を音読しよう ☐

📖 Reading 本文の内容を読んで理解しよう【知識・技能】【思考力・判断力・表現力】 共通テスト GTEC®

Make the correct choice to complete each sentence or answer each question. （各5点）

(1) Local governments are trying to use AI to ☐ .
  ① give their citizens better medical services
  ② give their doctors better medical services
  ③ give their visitors better medical services
  ④ give their workers better medical services

(2) What does "relieve" mean in line 6? ☐
  ① annoy   ② ease   ③ upset   ④ worry

(3) Which of the following is true? ☐
  ① As AI system is used in more fields, it will lower our quality of life.
  ② If AI is used successfully, we will be able to live well with it.
  ③ The AI system can cope with emergency cases after workers in emergency medical services do.
  ④ The AI system is helpful for workers in emergency medical services to increase their burdens.

🏷 Vocabulary & Grammar　重要表現や文法事項について理解しよう【知識】　　英検® GTEC®

Make the correct choice to complete each sentence.　（各3点）

(1)　Our teacher gave us (　　　) about how to improve our English.
　　① an advice　　　　　　　　　　② many advices
　　③ many pieces of advices　　　　④ some advice

(2)　Three of the candles went out one (　　　) another.
　　① after　　　　② for　　　　③ on　　　　④ with

(3)　The doctor knew how to cope (　　　) an emergency like this.
　　① for　　　　② in　　　　③ on　　　　④ with

(4)　Penicillin was one of the world's greatest (　　　) discoveries.
　　① hospital　　② hospitalize　　③ medical　　④ medicine

(5)　There are several reasons (　　　) we should not agree with her idea.
　　① because why　　② how　　③ which　　④ why

🎧 Listening　英文を聞いて理解しよう【知識・技能】【思考力・判断力・表現力】　　共通テスト　💿 54

Listen to the English and make the best choice to match the content.　（4点）
　　① Robots can cause some serious problems.
　　② Robots cannot become as clever as human beings.
　　③ We should teach robots as much knowledge as possible.

💬 Interaction　英文を聞いて会話を続けよう【知識・技能】【思考力・判断力・表現力】　スピーキング・トレーナー　💿 55

Listen to the English and respond to the last remark.　（7点）
　〔メ モ　　　　　　　　　　　　　　　　　　　　　　　　　　　　　　〕
🔑 **Hints**
英会話アプリの特徴を踏まえて話しましょう。

✏️ Production（Writing）　自分の考えを書いて伝えよう【思考力・判断力・表現力】

Write your answer to the following question.　（9点）
Do you think it is possible for human beings and AI to coexist? Why?

🔑 **Hints**
arithmetic（演算，計算能力），creative（創造的な），mutual（相互の）

Stop Microplastic Pollution!

Part 1
教科書 p.128-129   / 50

Manabu 2 hours ago //

This afternoon, / I went to a café / with Takashi. // I ordered some **iced** coffee / as usual, / but something was different / today. // The person / at the **counter** / didn't give me a plastic **straw**. // She said, / "We have stopped / serving
5 plastic straws / **globally**. // We want / to help / to save the environment / from **microplastic** pollution." //

What are microplastics? // I searched for information / about the microplastic problem / on the Internet, / and I learned / that it is becoming very serious. // I was shocked. // The government / in every country / should make its people /
10 stop wasting plastic products. //

Now, / I really want / to do something / to solve this problem. // Let's discuss the problem together. //

Takashi 30 minutes ago //

   We use a lot of plastics / every day. // Should we stop using them? //
15 Vivian 45 minutes ago //

   What can we do / about this? //

Kumi 1 hour ago //

   I had no idea / about this problem. //

(133 words)

🔊 **音読しよう** 📖 ～～～～～～～～～ スピーキング・トレーナー

Practice 1 スラッシュ位置で文を区切って読んでみよう ☐
Practice 2 音声を聞きながら，音声のすぐ後を追って読んでみよう ☐
TRY! 1分15秒以内に本文全体を音読しよう ☐

📖 **Reading** 本文の内容を読んで理解しよう【知識・技能】【思考力・判断力・表現力】   共通テスト

Make the correct choice to complete each sentence or answer each question. (各7点)

(1) Manabu claims that the government in every country should ☐ plastic products.
   ① encourage its people to waste   ② make its people quit overusing
   ③ prohibit its people from using   ④ try to recycle

(2) Which of the following is true? ☐
   ① Kumi didn't know about the microplastic problem.
   ② Manabu went to a café with Takashi and ordered some hot coffee.
   ③ Takashi wants to use plastic straws.
   ④ Vivian searched for information about the microplastic problem on the Internet.

Vocabulary & Grammar　重要表現や文法事項について理解しよう【知識】　英検® GTEC®

Make the correct choice to complete each sentence.　（各3点）

(1) Mike is never punctual. He was late for school today (　　　).
　① as usual　　　② as well as　　　③ in short　　　④ in the end

(2) Dinner will be (　　　) at 7 p.m.
　① accepted　　　② exchanged　　　③ reached　　　④ served

(3) UNIQLO has become a (　　　) recognized brand.
　① hardly　　　② globally　　　③ naturally　　　④ usually

(4) Let's (　　　) one more slice of pizza.
　① decide　　　② order　　　③ supply　　　④ want

(5) Please (　　　) what time will be convenient for you.
　① let know me　　　② let me know　　　③ let me to know　　　④ to let me know

Listening　英文を聞いて理解しよう【知識・技能】【思考力・判断力・表現力】　共通テスト　💿56

Listen to the English and make the best choice to match the content.　（5点）
　① The speaker always uses plastic bags when she goes shopping.
　② The speaker has her own reusable bag.
　③ The speaker usually goes shopping on weekends.

Interaction　英文を聞いて会話を続けよう【知識・技能】【思考力・判断力・表現力】　スピーキング・トレーナー　💿57

Listen to the English and respond to the last remark.　（7点）
　〔メ モ　　　　　　　　　　　　　　　　　　　　　　　　　　　　　　　〕

🔑**Hints**
　I like to use ... because ～の表現を使って話しましょう。

Production (Speaking)　自分の考えを話して伝えよう【思考力・判断力・表現力】　スピーキング・トレーナー

Answer the following question.　（9点）

What do you think should the Japanese government do to stop people from consuming plastic products too much?

　〔メ モ　　　　　　　　　　　　　　　　　　　　　　　　　　　　　　　〕

🔑**Hints**
　plastic bottled beverage（ペットボトル飲料），reusable bag（再利用できるバッグ），encourage ... to ～（…が～するように促す）

Lesson 9

Stop Microplastic Pollution!

When you walk / along the beach, / you may see a lot of small objects / shining in the **sand**. // Perhaps / they are "microplastics." //

"**Micro**" means "very small." // Microplastics are very small pieces / of plastic garbage. // They are less than about five **millimeters** / in **diameter**. // Plastics
5 easily break / into small pieces / when they are heated / or **exposed** / to **sunlight** / for a long time. //

Wood pieces and grass / on the beach / can be eaten / by **microbes**, / but plastics often **remain** there. // Plastics may become smaller, / but they do not disappear / easily. // Most of them / may be washed down / into the sea / and
10 stay there forever. // As a result, / the sea becomes the "dead end" / of the plastics / people throw away. //

(117 words)

 音読しよう   スピーキング・トレーナー

Practice 1 スラッシュ位置で文を区切って読んでみよう ☐
Practice 2 音声を聞きながら，音声のすぐ後を追って読んでみよう ☐
TRY! 1分5秒以内に本文全体を音読しよう ☐

Reading 本文の内容を読んで理解しよう【知識・技能】【思考力・判断力・表現力】   共通テスト GTEC®

Make the correct choice to complete each sentence or answer each question. （各5点）

(1) What does "expose" mean in line 5? ☐
  ① expect   ② protect   ③ solve   ④ uncover

(2) The sea becomes the "dead end" of the plastics people throw away because the plastics may be ☐ .
  ① eaten by microbes and disappear forever
  ② exposed to sunlight and break into small pieces
  ③ turned into microplastics for a week or so
  ④ washed down into the sea and stay there permanently

(3) Which of the following is true? ☐
  ① Not only wood pieces and grass but also plastics on the beach can be eaten by microbes.
  ② Plastics break into small pieces easily when they are exposed to sunshine for a long time.
  ③ The diameters of microplastics are over about five millimeters.
  ④ When you walk along the beach, you may see a lot of garbage on the sand.

意味の区切りを理解してスムーズに音読することができる。 ■ プラスチックに関する英文を読んで概要や要点をとらえることができる。

文脈を理解して適切な語句を用いて英文を完成することができる。 ■ 平易な英語で話される短い英文を聞いて必要な情報を聞き取ることができる。

海洋汚染について簡単な語句を用いて情報や考えを伝えることができる。 ■ ごみ問題について簡単な語句を用いて考えを表現することができる。

🗂 Vocabulary & Grammar 重要表現や文法事項について理解しよう【知識】 （英検®）（GTEC®）

Make the correct choice to complete each sentence. （各 3 点）

(1) By swimming alone, he (　　　) himself to danger.

① effected　　　② expected　　　③ experienced　　　④ exposed

(2) (　　　) the children in this school are under 11 years old.

① Most　　　② Most of　　　③ Most of all　　　④ The most

(3) He (　　　) silent for a long time.

① reduced　　　② refused　　　③ remained　　　④ reminded

(4) One of the most powerful cues to wake up the brain is (　　　).

① foundation　　　② information　　　③ sunlight　　　④ temperature

(5) I heard her (　　　) a song in the bathroom.

① having sung　　　② singing　　　③ sung　　　④ to sing

🎧 Listening 英文を聞いて理解しよう【知識・技能】【思考力・判断力・表現力】 （共通テスト）◉58

Listen to the English and make the best choice to match the content. （4 点）

① Eight tons of plastic garbage are washed down into the sea every year.

② Lots of plastic garbage is polluting the sea.

③ The amount of plastic garbage of this year is eight times as large as that of last year.

💬 Interaction 英文を聞いて会話を続けよう【知識・技能】【思考力・判断力・表現力】 スピーキング・トレーナー ◉59

Listen to the English and respond to the last remark. （7 点）

〔メモ 　　　　　　　　　　　　　　　　　　　　　　　　　　　　　〕

🔊 Hints
domestic wastewater (生活排水), oil stain (油汚れ), wipe (…を拭く)

✏ Production (Writing) 自分の考えを書いて伝えよう【思考力・判断力・表現力】

Write your answer to the following question. （9 点）

We should reduce the amount of garbage to save the environment. What can you do from the perspective of the 3Rs: Reduce, Reuse, and Recycle?

🔊 Hints
disposable (使い捨てできる), flea market (フリーマーケット), second-hand (中古の)

Stop Microplastic Pollution!

Microplastics are found / in the oceans / all over the world. // **According** to a study, / 2.4 pieces / of microplastics / were found / in every **ton** / of **seawater**, / even at several kilometers / away from the **coast**. // Now, / such **polluted** seawater / is called "plastic soup." //

5　Microplastics spread / through the food **chain**. // **Plankton** are near the bottom / of the food chain. // The plankton may eat microplastics / if they mistake them for their food. // Microplastic pollution spreads / as small fish eat plankton / and the bigger sea animals, / such as **sharks** and **whales**, / eat those small fish. //

Such a situation may be bad / for people's health / because people may eat fish / 10　that have eaten microplastics. // In fact, / plastics are found / within the fishes' bodies. //

(117 words)

 音読しよう

スピーキング・トレーナー

Practice 1 スラッシュ位置で文を区切って読んでみよう ☐
Practice 2 音声を聞きながら，音声のすぐ後を追って読んでみよう ☐
TRY! 1分10秒以内に本文全体を音読しよう ☐

Reading 本文の内容を読んで理解しよう【知識・技能】【思考力・判断力・表現力】 （共通テスト）

Make the correct choice to answer each question. （各7点）

(1) You are summarizing the information you have just studied. How should the table be finished? ☐

① (A) people 　　　　　　(B) small fish
　(C) bigger sea animals (D) plankton

② (A) people 　　　　　　(B) bigger sea animals
　(C) small fish 　　　　　(D) plankton

③ (A) plankton 　　　　　(B) bigger sea animals
　(C) small fish 　　　　　(D) people

④ (A) plankton 　　　　　(B) small fish
　(C) bigger sea animals (D) people

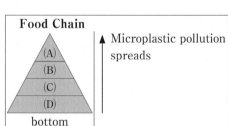

Food Chain

Microplastic pollution spreads

(A)
(B)
(C)
(D)
bottom

(2) Which of the following is true? ☐

① As small fish eat plankton and the bigger sea animals eat those small fish, microplastic pollution spreads.

② It isn't bad for people's health to eat fish which have eaten microplastics in the ocean.

③ Plankton exist at the top of the food chain.

④ Plankton never eat microplastics because they distinguish them from their food.

Vocabulary & Grammar 　重要表現や文法事項について理解しよう【知識】　　英検® ｜ GTEC®

Make the correct choice to complete each sentence. （各3点）

(1) (　　　　) to the weather forecast, it is going to rain tonight.

　① According　　　② Due　　　　　③ Owing　　　　④ Thanks

(2) I always mistake Chris (　　　　) her sister.　It's hard for me to tell them apart.

　① for　　　　　② on　　　　　　③ to　　　　　　④ with

(3) I don't like winter much.　In (　　　　), I really hate it.

　① addition to　　② advance　　　③ case　　　　④ fact

(4) People are at the top of food (　　　　).

　① agency　　　　② chain　　　　③ company　　　④ technology

(5) You can come and see me anytime if you (　　　　) free tomorrow.

　① are　　　　　② are going to be　③ were　　　　④ will be

🎧 Listening 　英文を聞いて理解しよう【知識・技能】【思考力・判断力・表現力】　　共通テスト ｜ 60

Listen to the English and make the best choice to match the content. （5点）

　① Human beings can affect microplastics.

　② Human beings may take in microplastics when they eat seafood.

　③ Microplastics are discovered around the world.

💬 Interaction 　英文を聞いて会話を続けよう【知識・技能】【思考力・判断力・表現力】　スピーキング・トレーナー ｜ 61

Listen to the English and respond to the last remark. （7点）

〔メモ 　　　　　　　　　　　　　　　　　　　　　　　　　　　　　　〕

🔖Hints

pick up garbage [trash]（ごみを拾う）, clean the beach（海岸をきれいにする）, litter（[場所を]ごみで散らかす）

🖊 Production（Writing） 　自分の考えを書いて伝えよう【思考力・判断力・表現力】

Write your answer to the following question. （9点）

Write about other examples of animals threatened by microplastics or plastic wastes.

🔖Hints

mistake A for B（A を B と間違える）, digestive system（消化器官）, entangle（…を絡めさせる）, fishing net（漁網）

More and more countries / have taken action / to solve the microplastic problem. // They have tried / to cut the amount / of plastic / people use. // They hope / that fewer plastic products will be used / around the world. //

Even young people can help / to solve the problem. // For example, / an
5　American girl made a **submarine** robot / to find microplastics / in the seawater. // Such robots may help / to clean the sea / in the future. //

Everybody can help / to change the situation. // You may say to yourself, / "Maybe / if I had a good idea, / I could do something useful." // However, / even if you don't have a very good idea, / you can say "no" / to some plastic products /
10　and make the problem less serious. // Let's act / for a brighter future. //

(124 words)

音読しよう　　　　　　　　　　　　　　スピーキング・トレーナー

Practice 1 スラッシュ位置で文を区切って読んでみよう ☐
Practice 2 音声を聞きながら，音声のすぐ後を追って読んでみよう ☐
TRY! 1分10秒以内に本文全体を音読しよう ☐

Reading 本文の内容を読んで理解しよう【知識・技能】【思考力・判断力・表現力】　(共通テスト)

Make the correct choice to complete each sentence or answer each question. （各5点［(3)は完答]）

(1) To solve the microplastic problem, more and more countries have tried to ☐.
① increase the amount of plastic people use
② increase the number of plastic products
③ make fewer plastic products
④ reduce the amount of plastic people use

(2) You have learned that a submarine robot can ☐.
① clean the sea　　　　　　　② cut the amount of plastic
③ find microplastics in the sea　　④ pick up microplastics in the seawater

(3) According to the article you read, which of the following are true? (Choose two options. The order does not matter.) ☐ · ☐
① A submarine robot which an American girl invented will be able to cut the amount of plastic people use.
② Everybody can help to solve the microplastic problem by saying "no" to some plastic products.
③ Few people are interested in the microplastic problem.
④ Young people can't help to solve the microplastic problem.
⑤ We don't need to come up with a very good idea to solve the microplastic problem.

🏷️ Vocabulary & Grammar 重要表現や文法事項について理解しよう【知識】 英検® GTEC®

Make the correct choice to complete each sentence. （各3点）

(1) The police are trained to deal with every (　　　) in a calm and professional manner.
　① condition 　　　　② information 　　　　③ situation 　　　　④ suggestion

(2) The mind can affect the body. (　　　), happy people tend to be healthy.
　① At once 　　　　② Even if 　　　　③ For example 　　　　④ In spite of

(3) We'll need to (　　　) quick action to avoid a crisis.
　① bring 　　　　② come 　　　　③ get 　　　　④ take

(4) "I want to be famous," he (　　　) to himself.
　① guessed 　　　　② said 　　　　③ supposed 　　　　④ told

(5) I (　　　) the offer if I were in your place.
　① will not accept 　　　　　　　　② will not have accepted
　③ would not accept 　　　　　　　④ would not have accepted

🎧 Listening 英文を聞いて理解しよう【知識・技能】【思考力・判断力・表現力】 共通テスト 💿62

Listen to the English and make the best choice to match the content. （4点）
　① Only a few used plastics are recycled all over the world.
　② People all over the world haven't taken any action to stop plastic pollution.
　③ Plastic pollution is one of the biggest problems in the world.

💬 Interaction 英文を聞いて会話を続けよう【知識・技能】【思考力・判断力・表現力】 スピーキング・トレーナー 💿63

Listen to the English and respond to the last remark. （7点）
　〔メ モ 　　　　　　　　　　　　　　　　　　　　　　　　　　　　　　　〕
🔑 **Hints**
　身の回りで行っている環境問題への取り組みを話しましょう。

✍️ Production (Writing) 自分の考えを書いて伝えよう【思考力・判断力・表現力】

Write your answer to the following question. （9点）
What should we do to cut the amount of plastic waste?

🔑 **Hints**
　プラスチックごみの削減に向けてできることを，3Rs (Reduce, Reuse, Recycle)の観点から考えてみましょう。

Jimmy Valentine was **released** / from **prison**, / and it was just a week later / that a safe was broken open / in Richmond, / Indiana. // Eight hundred dollars was **stolen**. // Two weeks after that, / a safe / in Logansport / was opened, / and fifteen hundred dollars / was taken. // Everyone was shocked, / as this safe was so strong / that people thought / no one could break it open. // Then a safe / in Jefferson City / was opened, / and five thousand dollars / was stolen. //

Ben Price was a **detective**. // He was a big man, / and famous for his skill / at solving very difficult and important cases. // So now / he began / to work / on these three cases. // He was the only person / who knew / how Jimmy did his job. // People / with safes / full of money / were glad / to hear / that Ben Price was at work / trying to **arrest** Mr. Valentine. //

One afternoon, / Jimmy Valentine and his suitcase / arrived in a small town / named Elmore. // Jimmy, / looking like an **athletic** young man / just home from college, / walked down the street / toward the hotel. //

A young lady walked / across the street, / passed him / at the corner, / and went through a door / with a sign / "The Elmore Bank" / on it. // Jimmy Valentine looked into her eyes, / forgot at once / what he was, / and became another man. // The young lady looked back at him, / and then **lowered** her eyes / as her face became red. // Handsome young men / like Jimmy / were not often seen / in Elmore. //

(241 words)

Practice 1 スラッシュ位置で文を区切って読んでみよう ☐
Practice 2 音声を聞きながら，音声のすぐ後を追って読んでみよう ☐
TRY! 2分20秒以内に本文全体を音読しよう ☐

スピーキング・トレーナー

Reading 本文の内容を読んで理解しよう【知識・技能】【思考力・判断力・表現力】　(共通テスト)

Make the correct choice to answer each question. （各5点）

(1) Which of the following is **not** suggested in the first paragraph? ☐
　① Everyone was shocked because Jimmy Valentine was released from prison.
　② Jimmy Valentine did his jobs soon after he was released from prison.
　③ Jimmy Valentine was a criminal who opened safes and stole money.
　④ Jimmy Valentine was very skillful at doing his job.

(2) Which of the following is **not** true about Ben Price? ☐
　① He had solved very difficult and important cases.
　② He knew how skillful Jimmy was at doing his job.
　③ He was a famous detective.
　④ He was well-known to people who had safes full of money.

Jimmy saw a boy / playing on the steps / of the bank / and began asking him questions / about the town. // After a time, / the young lady came out of the bank. // This time / she **pretended** / not to notice the young man / with the suitcase, / and went her way. // "Isn't that young lady Polly Simpson?" / Jimmy asked the boy. //

5　"No," / answered the boy. // "She's Annabel Adams. // Her father is the owner / of this bank." //

Jimmy went to the hotel. // He told the hotel clerk / that his name was Ralph D. Spencer, / and that he had come / to Elmore / to look for a place / where he could set up a shoe shop. // The clerk was so impressed / by Jimmy's clothes and **manner** / that he kindly gave him as
10　much information / about the town / as he could. // Yes, / Elmore needed a good shoe shop. // It was a **pleasant** town / to live in, / and the people were friendly. //

"Mr. Spencer" told the hotel clerk / that he would like to stay / in the town / for a few days / and look over the situation. // Mr. Ralph D. Spencer, / Jimmy Valentine's new **identity** / —— an identity / created by a sudden **attack** of love / —— remained in Elmore / and opened
15　a shoe shop. //

Soon / his shoe shop was doing a good business, / and he won the respect / of the **community**. // And more importantly, / he got to know Annabel Adams. // They fell deeply in love / and started / to plan their **wedding**. //

(239 words)

音読しよう　　　　　　　　　　　　　　　　　　　　　　　スピーキング・トレーナー

Practice 1　スラッシュ位置で文を区切って読んでみよう ☐
Practice 2　音声を聞きながら，音声のすぐ後を追って読んでみよう ☐
TRY!　2分20秒以内に本文全体を音読しよう ☐

Reading　本文の内容を読んで理解しよう【知識・技能】【思考力・判断力・表現力】　　共通テスト

Make the correct choice to complete each sentence or answer each question.　（各5点[(2)は完答]）

(1) Jimmy asked a boy questions about the town to ☐.
　① break open the safe of the bank and steal money
　② get more information about it
　③ get some information about the young lady
　④ set up a shoe shop in the town

(2) According to the story you read, which of the following are true? (Choose two options. The order does not matter.) ☐ ・ ☐
　① Jimmy had come to Elmore to set up a shoe shop.
　② Jimmy won not only the respect of the people in Elmore but also the love of Annabel Adams.
　③ Soon Jimmy's shoe shop was doing a good business, but he found it hard to be accepted by the community.
　④ The flame of a sudden attack of love had made Jimmy quite another man.
　⑤ The hotel clerk gave Jimmy as much information as he could under the impression that Jimmy was just a rich tourist.

One day, / Jimmy wrote a letter / to one of his old friends / in Little Rock. // The letter said, / "I want / to give you my tools. // You couldn't buy them / even for a thousand dollars. // I don't need them anymore / because I finished with the old business / a year ago. // I will never touch another man's money / again." //

5　It was a few days / after Jimmy sent his letter / that Ben Price **secretly** arrived / in Elmore. // He went around the town / in his quiet way / until he found out all / he wanted to know. // From a drugstore / across the street / from Spencer's shoe shop, / he watched Ralph D. Spencer / walk by. // "You think / you're going to marry the **banker**'s daughter, / don't you, / Jimmy?" / said Ben / to himself, / softly. // "Well, / I'm not so sure / about that!" //

10　The next morning, / Jimmy had breakfast / at the Adams home. // That day, / he was going to Little Rock / to order his wedding **suit**, / buy something nice / for Annabel, / and give his tools away / to his friend. //

After breakfast, / several members / of the Adams family / went to the bank together / —— Mr. Adams, / Annabel, / Jimmy, / and Annabel's married sister / with her two little

15　girls, / aged five and nine. // On the way to the bank, / they waited / outside Jimmy's shop / while he ran up to his room / and got his suitcase. // Then / they went on / to the bank. //

(228 words)

🔊)) 音読しよう　📖 ～～～～～～～～～～～～～～～～～～　スピーキング・トレーナー

Practice 1 スラッシュ位置で文を区切って読んでみよう ☐
Practice 2 音声を聞きながら，音声のすぐ後を追って読んでみよう ☐
TRY! 2分10秒以内に本文全体を音読しよう ☐

📖 Reading　本文の内容を読んで理解しよう【知識・技能】【思考力・判断力・表現力】　　共通テスト

Make the correct choice to complete each sentence or answer each question. （各5点）

(1) Jimmy's letter to his old friend said that ☐.
　① he had finished with his old job
　② he was waiting for his friend to come to Elmore
　③ he would buy his tools for a thousand dollars
　④ he would close his shoe shop and retire from the business world

(2) What was in "his suitcase"? ☐
　① His tools for breaking safes open.
　② His wedding suit, and something nice for Annabel.
　③ Letters from his old friends in Little Rock.
　④ Money he had stolen from safes.

They all went into the **banking-room** / —— Jimmy, / too, / for Mr. Adams' future **son-in-law** / was welcome / anywhere. // Everyone in the bank / was glad / to see the **good-looking**, nice young man / who was going to marry Annabel. // Jimmy put down the suitcase / in the corner / of the room. //

5　The Elmore Bank had just put in a new safe. // It was as large as a small room / and it had a very special new kind of door / that was **controlled** / by a clock. // Mr. Adams was very proud of this new safe / and was showing / how to set the time / when the door should open. // The two children, / May and Agatha, / enjoyed touching all the interesting parts / of its shining heavy door. //

10　While these things were happening, / Ben Price quietly entered the bank / and looked inside the banking-room. // He told the bank **teller** / that he didn't want anything; / he was just waiting / for a man / he knew. //

Suddenly, / there were **screams** / from the women. // May, / the five-year-old girl, / had **firmly** closed the door / of the safe / by accident, / and Agatha was inside! // Mr. Adams tried hard / 15 to pull open the door / for a moment, / and then cried, / "The door can't be opened! // And the clock / —— I haven't started it / yet." //

"Please break it open!" / Agatha's mother cried out. //

"Quiet!" / said Mr. Adams, / raising a shaking hand. // "Everyone, / be quiet / for a moment. // Agatha!" / he called as loudly / as he could. // "Can you hear me?" // They could hear, / 20 **although** not clearly, / the sound / of the child's voice. // In the **darkness** / inside the safe, / she was screaming / with **fear**. // Agatha's mother, / now getting more **desperate**, / started hitting the door / with her hands. //

(277 words)

音読しよう 📖　　　　　　　　　　　　　　　　スピーキング・トレーナー

Practice 1 スラッシュ位置で文を区切って読んでみよう ☐
Practice 2 音声を聞きながら，音声のすぐ後を追って読んでみよう ☐
TRY! 2分40秒以内に本文全体を音読しよう ☐

📖 Reading 本文の内容を読んで理解しよう【知識・技能】【思考力・判断力・表現力】　（共通テスト）

Make the correct choice to answer each question. （各5点[(1)は完答]）

(1) According to the story you read, which of the following are <u>not</u> true? (Choose two options. The order does not matter.) ☐・☐
① Ben Price was waiting for a man who could tell that "Mr. Spencer" was Jimmy Valentine.
② Ben Price was watching all the things which were happening in the banking-room.
③ Everybody in the bank knew what Mr. Adams' future son-in-law was like.
④ Jimmy was treated as if he were already a member of the Adams family.
⑤ The new safe of the Elmore bank had a special door controlled by a clock.

(2) Suddenly, there were screams from the women. (*l.*13) What happened? ☐
① Agatha, the nine-year-old girl, began to scream with fear.
② Agatha was locked in the safe.
③ May, the five-year-old girl, closed the door of the safe.
④ Mr. Adams started the clock by accident.

Annabel turned to Jimmy. // Her large eyes were full of **pain**, / but not yet **despairing**. // A woman believes / that the man / she loves / can find a way / to do anything. // "Can't you do something, / Ralph? // Try, / won't you?" // He looked at her / with a strange, soft smile / on his lips / and in his eyes. //

5　"Annabel," / he said, / "give me that rose / you are wearing, / will you?" //

She couldn't understand / what he meant, / but she put the rose / in his hand. // Jimmy took it / and placed it / in the pocket / of his **vest**. // Then / he threw off his coat. // With that act, / Ralph D. Spencer disappeared, / and Jimmy Valentine took his place. // "Stay away from the door, / all of you," / he ordered. //

10　He placed his suitcase / on the table / and opened it. // From that time on, / he didn't pay any attention / to anyone else there. // Quickly / he laid the strange shining tools / on the table. // Nobody moved / as they watched him work. // Soon / Jimmy's **drill** was **biting smoothly** / into the **steel** door. // In ten minutes / —— faster / than he had ever done it before / —— he opened the door. //

15　Agatha, / **completely exhausted** / but **unharmed**, / ran into her mother's arms. // Jimmy Valentine silently put his coat back on / and walked / toward the front door / of the bank. // As he went, / he thought / he heard a voice call, / "Ralph!" // But he never **hesitated**. // At the door, / a big man was standing / in his way. // "Hello, / Ben!" / said Jimmy. // "You're here / at last, / aren't you? // Well, / let's go. // I don't care now." //

20　"I'm afraid / you're mistaken, / Mr. Spencer," / said Ben Price. // "I don't believe / I recognize you." // Then / the big detective turned away / and walked slowly down the street. //

(283 words)

🔊)) 音読しよう 📖 ～～～～～～～～～～～～～ スピーキング・トレーナー

Practice 1　スラッシュ位置で文を区切って読んでみよう ☐
Practice 2　音声を聞きながら，音声のすぐ後を追って読んでみよう ☐
TRY!　2分40秒以内に本文全体を音読しよう ☐

📖 Reading　本文の内容を読んで理解しよう【知識・技能】【思考力・判断力・表現力】　(共通テスト)

Make the correct choice to complete each sentence. (各5点)

(1) When he asked Annabel for the rose she was wearing, Jimmy clearly saw in his mind that ☐.

① he would be able to save Agatha　　② he would be arrested by Ben Price
③ he would have to say goodbye to her　④ he would start a new life with her

(2) When he said, "Hello, Ben!", Jimmy ☐.

① expected Ben to let him go
② expected that Ben would not recognize him
③ was ready to be arrested by Ben
④ was surprised to see Ben there

Ask Friends and Followers for Advice on Social Media

教科書 p. 156 　　/ 15

Nyanko //

Our **brass** band practice is very hard / every day. // After practice, / I ride on the train / for about one hour / and get home late. // After I eat dinner / and take a bath, / it is already 9:30 p.m. // I'm always tired and sleepy! // How can I

5　study? // Please give me some good advice. //

Yujin: Use your **spare** time **wisely**. // For example, / you can study / while you are on the train. //

Ribrib: Why don't you get up early / and study / in the early morning? // I do it. // It's really **refreshing**. //

10　David: You should tell your teacher / and other band members / about your problem. // They may give you good advice. //

(108 words)

🔊)) 音読しよう 📖 ～～～～～～～～～～～～～～～～ スピーキング・トレーナー

Practice 1 スラッシュ位置で文を区切って読んでみよう ☐
Practice 2 音声を聞きながら，音声のすぐ後を追って読んでみよう ☐
TRY! 1分以内に本文全体を音読しよう ☐

📖 **Reading** 本文の内容を読んで理解しよう【知識・技能】【思考力・判断力・表現力】　　共通テスト

Make the correct choice to complete each sentence or answer each question. (各5点)

(1) It is difficult for Nyanko to ☐.
① be always tired and sleepy
② eat dinner and take a bath every day
③ have enough time to study
④ ride on the train for about one hour

(2) Who advises Nyanko to study in the early morning? ☐
① David　　　　　　　　　　② Ribrib
③ the brass band members　　④ Yujin

(3) Which of the following is true? ☐
① David advises Nyanko to quit the brass band.
② Nyanko says that it is important to study hard every day.
③ Ribrib studies in the early morning.
④ Yujin advises Nyanko to study while she rides on the bus.

Let's Buy Fair-trade Chocolate!

教科書 p. 157   / 15

You Can Make a Difference / in Farmers' Lives! //

Chocolate may be your favorite food. // But do you know / growing cacao trees / is hard work? // Cacao trees grow / in hot, rainy, **tropical** places. // Cacao plants are **delicate**. //

5   Small family farmers grow about 90% / of the world's cacao. // They must protect trees / from wind, / sun, / insects / and **illness**. // Cacao prices are rising, / but the farmers get very little / from its **trade**. // The **traders** take away / much of the **profit**. //

Thanks to fair-trade, / cacao farming can be **sustainable**. // We buy cacao
10 beans / from those small farmers / at fair prices. // We set up local **funds**, / too. // Fair-trade has rules / about farming / to protect the environment. //

Why don't you buy fair-trade chocolate? // That can be a great help / for cacao farmers. //

(126 words)

音読しよう   スピーキング・トレーナー

Practice 1 スラッシュ位置で文を区切って読んでみよう ☐
Practice 2 音声を聞きながら，音声のすぐ後を追って読んでみよう ☐
TRY! 1分10秒以内に本文全体を音読しよう ☐

Reading   本文の内容を読んで理解しよう【知識・技能】【思考力・判断力・表現力】   共通テスト GTEC®

Make the correct choice to complete each sentence or answer each question. （各5点）

(1) Farmers must protect cacao trees from wind, sun, insects and illness because [____].
   ① cacao plants are delicate
   ② cacao plants grow in rainy places
   ③ cacao plants grow in tropical places
   ④ cacao prices are rising

(2) Buying fair-trade chocolate is good because [____].
   ① cacao farmers can get little profit
   ② it helps make cacao farming sustainable
   ③ traders can take away much of the profit
   ④ we can buy cacao beans from small farmers at low prices

(3) What does "sustainable" mean in line 9? [____]
   ① continuable   ② effective   ③ important   ④ useful

Good to Be Different

教科書 p. 158　　　／ 15

Reporter: What was the Rio Paralympics like / for you? //

Mei: I felt relieved / when I was chosen / for the Japanese team. // People hoped / I could get a medal, / but I knew / I wasn't good enough. //

Reporter: After Rio, / you trained / in Australia / for three months. // What did
5　you learn there? //

Mei: Before that, / I just tried hard / to get a good result. // On the other hand, / Australian swimmers focused / on the quality / of their swimming. // I learned / to think **logically** / about my own performance, / and not just **rely** too much / on feelings. //

10　*Reporter:* Who had an impact / on your way / of thinking? //

Mei: My mom and dad. // They told me / it's good / to be different. // I hope / people see each person / as an individual. //

(118 words)

🔊 **音読しよう** 　　　　　　　　　　　　　　　　　スピーキング・トレーナー

Practice 1 スラッシュ位置で文を区切って読んでみよう ☐
Practice 2 音声を聞きながら，音声のすぐ後を追って読んでみよう ☐
TRY! 1分5秒以内に本文全体を音読しよう ☐

📖 Reading 　本文の内容を読んで理解しよう【知識・技能】【思考力・判断力・表現力】　　　共通テスト

Make the correct choice to complete each sentence or answer each question. （各5点）

(1) Before training in Australia, Mei practiced swimming hard to ☐ .

① get a good result

② improve the quality of her swimming

③ rely on her feelings

④ think logically about her performance

(2) ☐ had an impact on Mei's way of thinking.

① Australian swimmers　　　　　② Her parents

③ Japanese swimmers　　　　　④ Only her mother

(3) Which of the following is true? ☐

① Australian swimmers focused on the quality of their swimming.

② Before Rio, Mei went to Australia and trained hard there.

③ Mei believed that she could get a gold medal at the Rio Paralympics.

④ Mei got a medal at the Rio Paralympics.

Dream Matches / Asian HS Tournament /
by Sakura Gaming Online / — July 20 //

Welcome to Dream Matches, / Asian HS Tournament / by Sakura Gaming. // This is a tournament / for Asian high school students / of all skill levels. // We 5 are looking forward / to seeing the fighting spirit / of all players. // We thank you / for **participating** / in this exciting event! //

Date & Time: / Match 1 | July 20, 2021 | 6 p.m. //

Match 2 | July 20, 2021 | 7 p.m. //

Structure: / 25 Teams | 1 match //

10 **Timezone**: / Tokyo (UTC+ 9:00) //

Fees: / Free to play matches //

Rules: / 1. Each team needs at least eight players / to participate. //

2. All players / in the tournament / must have ESPORTS **accounts**. //

3. Players must not use / any **unofficial versions** / of games. //

15 4. Players must not use / unofficial items. //

5. All team players must **register** / by the **deadline**. //

After **registration**, / players will get more information / about the event. //

Registration is now open / and will run / until July 20, / 2021, / 4 p.m. / JST. //

(155 words)

🔊)) 音読しよう 📖 〜〜〜〜〜〜〜〜〜〜〜〜 スピーキング・トレーナー

Practice 1 スラッシュ位置で文を区切って読んでみよう ☐
Practice 2 音声を聞きながら，音声のすぐ後を追って読んでみよう ☐
TRY! 1分25秒以内に本文全体を音読しよう ☐

📖 **Reading** 本文の内容を読んで理解しよう【知識・技能】【思考力・判断力・表現力】 (共通テスト)

Make the correct choice to complete each sentence or answer each question. (各5点[(2)は完答])

(1) You have learned that players in this tournament have to ☐.

① pay the participation fee ② play individual matches

③ register by July 20, 2021, 6 p.m. ④ use official items

(2) According to the website you read, which of the following are true? (Choose two options. The order does not matter.) ☐・☐

① Asian high school students of all skill levels play matches in this tournament.

② Dream Matches will be held in Tokyo.

③ High school students around the world can take part in this tournament.

④ Match 1 will be held in July 20, 2021, 4 p.m.

⑤ Players have to use official versions of games.

"Favorite" Encounters

教科書 p. 160 ☐ / 15

I was born / to an American father / and a Japanese mother. // I went to Yokohama International School. // Sometimes / it was **challenging** / for me / to communicate / in English / at school. // I first **encountered** the *koto* / at the age of nine. // I loved playing the musical **instrument** / during my first Japanese

5 music classes / because I could make beautiful sounds / with it / easily. //

I was first taught / by Mr. Patterson. // He has lived / in Japan / since 1986 / and performs / and teaches the *koto*. // He is a great teacher. //

My classmates were impressed / with my playing / and this encouraged me / to work harder. // I realized / that it was easier / to **express** myself / through

10 the *koto* / than with words. //

I became a professional *koto* player / in 2017, / and now / I enjoy **collaborating** / with various artists. //

(130 words)

🔊 音読しよう 📖 ～～～～～～～～～～～～ スピーキング・トレーナー

Practice 1 スラッシュ位置で文を区切って読んでみよう ☐
Practice 2 音声を聞きながら，音声のすぐ後を追って読んでみよう ☐
TRY! 1分15秒以内に本文全体を音読しよう ☐

📖 Reading 本文の内容を読んで理解しよう【知識・技能】【思考力・判断力・表現力】 共通テスト GTEC®

Make the correct choice to complete each sentence or answer each question. (各5点[(3)は完答])

(1) What does "encounter" mean in line 3? ☐
　① come about 　　② come across 　　③ come after 　　④ come away

(2) Leo liked playing the *koto* when he was a child. That was because ☐ .
　① a great teacher taught him the *koto*
　② he loved Japanese music classes at school
　③ it was easy for him to communicate in English
　④ it was easy for him to make beautiful sounds with the instrument

(3) According to the post you read, which of the following are true? (Choose two options. The order does not matter.) ☐ · ☐
　① Leo found it easier to express himself through the *koto* than with words.
　② Leo is a professional *koto* player and enjoys playing together with various artists.
　③ Leo was born in America.
　④ Leo was good at communicating in English because he went to Yokohama International School.
　⑤ Mr. Patterson is a teacher who teaches English at Yokohama International School.

Japanese Students Appeal for World Peace

教科書 p. 161 　　／ 15

Japanese High School Students / Go to the U.N. //

Do you think / young people have the power / to change the world? // Now, / the world knows / that some Japanese high school students / have worked hard / to help / to create a **peaceful** world. //

5　Japanese High School Student Peace **Ambassadors** / are chosen / every year / from around the country. // They **attend** many **conferences**, / including one / at the United Nations Office. // There, / they make speeches / in English / to appeal for world peace. // They also **submit signatures** / they have collected / in support of the **abolition** / of **nuclear weapons**. //

10　In addition, / the ambassadors do some charity activities. // They collect pencils and other **stationery**, / and they send them / to some poor countries. // They also run a charity fund / for poor children / in Asia. //

In total, / more than 200 students / have worked hard / for peace / since 1998. // Their voices have reached many people / around the world. //

(146 words)

🔊) 音読しよう 📖 ～～～～～～～～～～ スピーキング・トレーナー

Practice 1 スラッシュ位置で文を区切って読んでみよう ☐
Practice 2 音声を聞きながら，音声のすぐ後を追って読んでみよう ☐
TRY! 1分20秒以内に本文全体を音読しよう ☐

📖 Reading 本文の内容を読んで理解しよう【知識・技能】【思考力・判断力・表現力】 共通テスト GTEC®

Make the correct choice to complete each sentence or answer each question. (各5点)

(1) Japanese High School Student Peace Ambassadors ☐.
　① are selected every year from all over the world
　② don't need to attend conferences
　③ have worked hard for more than 200 years
　④ have worked hard to create a peaceful world

(2) What does "conference" mean in line 6? ☐
　① agreement　　　② discovery　　　③ lecture　　　④ meeting

(3) What will you do if you are chosen as a member of Japanese High School Student Peace Ambassadors? ☐
　① Buy pencils and other stationery and send them to poor countries.
　② Collect signatures in support of the abolition of nuclear weapons.
　③ Make speeches in English to promote the use of nuclear weapons.
　④ Run a charity fund for poor children all over the world.

The number of convenience stores / in Japan / has been growing. // Convenience stores are easy / to drop into. // Their products are **constantly** changing. // Every year, / about 70% / of all products / are **replaced** / by new ones. // This is / because of demand / from society. //

5 The customers of convenience stores / used to be mainly young people, / but these days, / that is not the case. // According to the graph, / in 2017, / the number of customers / aged 50 or over / was four times / as large as that / in 1989. //

There will be more and more elderly people / in the future. // Home **delivery** of products / will become more common / for people / who cannot travel easily. //

10 They can order what they need online / and get it / at home. // As our society is changing, / the meaning of "convenience" / can also change. //

(132 words)

🔊 **音読しよう** 📖 スピーキング・トレーナー

Practice 1 スラッシュ位置で文を区切って読んでみよう ☐
Practice 2 音声を聞きながら，音声のすぐ後を追って読んでみよう ☐
TRY! 1分15秒以内に本文全体を音読しよう ☐

📖 **Reading** 本文の内容を読んで理解しよう【知識・技能】【思考力・判断力・表現力】 (共通テスト)

Make the correct choice to complete each sentence or answer each question. (各5点[(2)は完答])

(1) You have learned that ☐ .
  ① about 70% of Japanese people drop into convenience stores
  ② about 70% of the convenience stores in Japan have disappeared
  ③ lots of products at convenience stores are constantly changing
  ④ the number of convenience stores in Japan will decrease in the future

(2) According to the article you read, which of the following are true? (Choose two options. The order does not matter.) ☐ · ☐
  ① Home delivery of products will be useful for people who cannot travel easily.
  ② Home delivery of products will enable us to order what we want online and get it at home.
  ③ Home delivery of products won't become common because convenience stores are easy to drop into.
  ④ The customers of convenience stores used to be mainly elderly people.
  ⑤ The meaning of "convenience" won't change because our society is unchangeable.

Machine Translation: No Need to Learn English?

教科書 p. 163　　／ 10

Machine **translation** is simple. // The machine **statistically** finds out the most **appropriate** match / from translation **data**. // A set of data / is like: / "髪が長くなった; / My hair got longer." // It is broken up / into smaller pieces, / such as "髪; / my hair" / and "長くなった; / got longer." // When you put "日が長くなった" /
5　into machine translation, / the machine matches the best pieces / of data / and produces "The day got longer." //

However, / machine translation has several problems. // If **translated** sentences are **inaccurate**, / we must correct them. // In addition, / it is sometimes difficult / for us / to recognize inaccurate translations. //
10　If we take an example, / like "部活で帰りが遅くなった," / we can see / how inaccurate sometimes machine translation is. //

部活で帰りが遅くなった。⇒ My return got late in club activities. //

This machine translation is very **unnatural**. // You should say, / "I returned home late / because of my club activities." // So / it is still important / for us / to
15　keep learning English hard. //

(139 words)

🔊 **音読しよう** 📖　　　　　　　　　　　　　　　　スピーキング・トレーナー

Practice 1 スラッシュ位置で文を区切って読んでみよう ☐
Practice 2 音声を聞きながら，音声のすぐ後を追って読んでみよう ☐
TRY! 1分15秒以内に本文全体を音読しよう ☐

📖 Reading　本文の内容を読んで理解しよう【知識・技能】【思考力・判断力・表現力】　　共通テスト

Make the correct choice to complete each sentence or answer each question. （各5点）

(1) You have learned that machine translation ☐.
　① finds the most appropriate match from dictionaries
　② finds the most appropriate match from translation data and translates Japanese into English
　③ is so complicated that Japanese students shouldn't use it when they study English
　④ only has advantages for English learners

(2) To describe the author's position, which of the following is most appropriate? ☐
　① The author believes machine translation always translates Japanese into English correctly.
　② The author encourages us to keep learning English because machine translation isn't always correct.
　③ The author states that we don't need to study English hard thanks to machine translation.
　④ The author suggests that we upgrade the quality of machine translation.

A Boy Helps to Solve the Microplastic Problem

教科書 p. 164　　　　/ 10

A Boy's **Discovery** / May Solve the Microplastic Problem //

　　Microplastic pollution is a **worldwide** problem today. //　A Canadian boy / has given us a good answer / to it. //　Daniel Burd, / a 16-year-old high school student, / showed his research / on microbes / that could eat plastics. //　He won
5　the top prize / at the Canada-Wide Science Fair. //

　　Daniel said, / "Plastics finally break down / and disappear, / though it usually takes 1,000 years / to do so. //　This means / some microbes can eat plastics slowly." //　Then / he asked himself, / "Can I make those microbes / do the job faster?" //　He did his **experiment** / again and again. //　At last, / he found the
10　most powerful type / of microbe. //

　　About 500 **billion** plastic bags / are used / worldwide / each year. //　Billions of these end up / in the oceans. //　Animals eat those plastic bags, / and as a result, / the animals often die. //　Daniel's discovery will help us / solve the microplastic problem. //

(147 words)

音読しよう　　　　　　　　　　　　　　　　　　　　　　　　スピーキング・トレーナー

Practice 1　スラッシュ位置で文を区切って読んでみよう ☐
Practice 2　音声を聞きながら，音声のすぐ後を追って読んでみよう ☐
TRY!　1分25秒以内に本文全体を音読しよう ☐

Reading　本文の内容を読んで理解しよう【知識・技能】【思考力・判断力・表現力】　　(共通テスト)

Make the correct choice to complete each sentence or answer each question.　(各5点[(2)は完答])

(1)　Daniel did his experiment and found the most powerful type of microbe that
　　☐.
　　① can eat microbes fast　　　　　　② can eat microplastics slowly
　　③ can eat plastic bags slowly　　　　④ can eat plastics fast

(2)　According to the website you read, which of the following are true?　(Choose two options.　The order does not matter.)　☐ · ☐
　　① A Canadian high school student got the top prize at the Canada-Wide Science Fair.
　　② About 500 billion plastic bags are washed into the oceans each year.
　　③ Animals that live in the oceans often die from eating plastic bags.
　　④ Daniel found that about 500 billion plastic bags are used in the world every year.
　　⑤ It will take 1,000 years to solve microplastic pollution.

WPM・得点一覧表

●スピーキング・トレーナーを使って，各レッスンの本文を流暢に音読できるようにしましょう。
下の計算式を使って，1分あたりに音読できた語数 (words per minute) を算出してみましょう。

【本文語数】÷【音読にかかった時間 (秒)】×60 ＝ ☐wpm

Lesson		WPM	得点
1	Part 1	/ wpm	/ 50
	Part 2	/ wpm	/ 50
	Part 3	/ wpm	/ 50
	流暢さの目安	70wpm	/ 150

Lesson		WPM	得点
2	Part 1	/ wpm	/ 50
	Part 2	/ wpm	/ 50
	Part 3	/ wpm	/ 50
	流暢さの目安	70wpm	/ 150

Lesson		WPM	得点
3	Part 1	/ wpm	/ 50
	Part 2	/ wpm	/ 50
	Part 3	/ wpm	/ 50
	流暢さの目安	70wpm	/ 150

Lesson		WPM	得点
4	Part 1	/ wpm	/ 50
	Part 2	/ wpm	/ 50
	Part 3	/ wpm	/ 50
	流暢さの目安	80wpm	/ 150

Lesson		WPM	得点
5	Part 1	/ wpm	/ 50
	Part 2	/ wpm	/ 50
	Part 3	/ wpm	/ 50
	流暢さの目安	80wpm	/ 150

Lesson		WPM	得点
6	Part 1	/ wpm	/ 50
	Part 2	/ wpm	/ 50
	Part 3	/ wpm	/ 50
	Part 4	/ wpm	/ 50
	流暢さの目安	80wpm	/ 200

Lesson		WPM	得点
7	Part 1	/ wpm	/ 50
	Part 2	/ wpm	/ 50
	Part 3	/ wpm	/ 50
	Part 4	/ wpm	/ 50
	流暢さの目安	90wpm	/ 200

Lesson		WPM	得点
8	Part 1	/ wpm	/ 50
	Part 2	/ wpm	/ 50
	Part 3	/ wpm	/ 50
	Part 4	/ wpm	/ 50
	流暢さの目安	90wpm	/ 200

Lesson		WPM	得点
9	Part 1	/ wpm	/ 50
	Part 2	/ wpm	/ 50
	Part 3	/ wpm	/ 50
	Part 4	/ wpm	/ 50
	流暢さの目安	100wpm	/ 200

Optional		WPM	得点
	Part 1	/ wpm	/ 10
	Part 2	/ wpm	/ 10
	Part 3	/ wpm	/ 10
	Part 4	/ wpm	/ 10
	Part 5	/ wpm	/ 10
	流暢さの目安	100wpm	/ 50

Additional	WPM	得点
Lesson 1	/ wpm	/ 15
Lesson 2	/ wpm	/ 15
Lesson 3	/ wpm	/ 15
Lesson 4	/ wpm	/ 10
Lesson 5	/ wpm	/ 15
Lesson 6	/ wpm	/ 15
Lesson 7	/ wpm	/ 10
Lesson 8	/ wpm	/ 10
Lesson 9	/ wpm	/ 10
流暢さの目安	100wpm	